PULLING OFF THE SHEETS

T0243789

Pulling off the Sheets

The Second Ku Klux Klan in
Deep Southern Illinois

Darrel Dexter
and
John A. Beadles

SOUTHERN ILLINOIS UNIVERSITY PRESS

CARBONDALE

Southern Illinois University Press
www.siupress.com

Printed in the United States of America

27 26 25 24   4 3 2 1

Cover illustration: Shutterstock photo 345923423 by AfriramPOE
(colorized and manipulated).

Library of Congress Cataloging-in-Publication Data

Names: Dexter, Darrel, 1962– author. | Beadles, John A., author.
Title: Pulling off the sheets : the second ku klux klan in deep southern illinois
  / Darrel Dexter and John A. Beadles.
Identifiers: LCCN 2023034612 (print) | LCCN 2023034613 (ebook) |
  ISBN 9780809339426 (paperback) | ISBN 9780809339433 (ebook)
Subjects: LCSH: Ku Klux Klan (1915–)—History—20th century. | Working class African
  Americans—Illinois | African Americans—Civil rights—Illinois. | Illinois—Race
  relations—History—20th century. | BISAC: HISTORY / United States / State & Local
  / Midwest (IA, IL, IN, KS, MI, MN, MO, ND, NE, OH, SD, WI) | SOCIAL SCIENCE
  / DiscriminationClassification: LCC HS2330.K63 D49 2024(print) |
  LCC HS2330.K63(ebook) | DDC 322.4/209773909042—dc23/eng/20231204
LC record available at https://lccn.loc.gov/2023034612
LC ebook record available at https://lccn.loc.gov/2023034613

Printed on recycled paper ♻

SIU
Southern Illinois University System

CONTENTS

Gallery of illustrations begins on page 71

PULLING OFF THE SHEETS

Prologue

WHEN I WAS GROWING UP in Ullin, Illinois, the silent ghosts of the Ku Klux Klan were unknowingly all around me. The first house I lived in as a child was less than half a mile from the site of a large Klan rally in 1924, and I went by the site almost daily with no realization of its historical significance. Many times, as a teenager I visited the house where my aunt lived near Elco, Illinois, not knowing it was the same house visited by Klan sympathizers in 1924 bent on forcing Black residents to move from the area. I never heard my parents, grandparents, or any relatives talk about the Klan having once existed in the area. If they knew about it, they were indifferent to it or did not want me to know about it. In fact, in doing research for this book, I found few current residents of Pulaski or Alexander County who remembered even hearing talk about the Klan in the area, although events discussed in this book were only a generation or two removed from most of them.

I was surprised to see the regional and family connections to the Klan, although as far as I know none of my ancestors were members of the Ku Klux Klan. Ben Sowers, a Methodist Episcopal minister and one of the organizers of the Klan in southern Illinois, was a childhood sweetheart of my grandmother, Ella Mowery, and they were once engaged to be married. She was a second cousin to Sheriff Ira Hudson, who resisted the Klan in Pulaski County in the 1920s. When she married my grandfather, Ben Dexter, in 1914, the ceremony was performed at Jonesboro by the Reverend Isaac Edward Lee, a Baptist minister who later became connected with the Klan in Williamson County.[1] The Reverend Charles L. Phifer, my grandparents' pastor at Beech Grove Methodist Episcopal Church, where I also attended as a child, was one of the local organizers of the Second Ku Klux Klan in the Ullin area. The

Klan's past was hiding all around me but never mentioned, whether out of forgetfulness or shame I am not certain.

As a child I heard the doctrine of White supremacy spoken in knowing whispers. Arch Miller, a farmer between Ullin and Elco, gave my father, Paul Dexter, his first job after high school, and my father laughingly told me how shocked and angry his mother was when she found out that "Uncle Arch" not only hired Black workers but allowed them to eat dinner at the same table with her son and the Miller family. My uncle remembered overhearing his parents arguing one night about my grandfather hiring Black workers to help on the farm after my father left home to enlist in the United States Navy during World War II. Two generations later, we were taught and conditioned to hide any ideas of White supremacy, as by the 1970s and 1980s such sentiments were not as publicly acceptable or politically correct. They are still prevalent but they have become covert, and perhaps that makes them even more dangerous and harder to confront. They are hidden beneath the sheets we often use to cover the past.

The evidence of race hatred and White supremacy in southern Illinois in the early 1900s is overwhelming. Nevertheless, just as there are those who would deny the existence of the Holocaust in Europe, there are those today who deny or choose to ignore the significance of the history of racism and racial violence in deep southern Illinois and more broadly in America as a whole. Such a denial and a desire to forget the racist past is itself often unknowingly steeped in racism. Healing does not occur because people forget; it only happens when everyone embraces the truth of past events and moves forward together.

This book is a history of a series of atrocities committed against one group of Americans by another group of Americans. The purpose of telling the story is not to make anyone feel guilty, as those who might have reason to feel remorse about the events presented here have been dead for decades. The authors have a strong faith in the belief that people are capable of growth and change and that many have grown and moved beyond their unchecked racism. An example of such change can be found in another pastor of Beech Grove and Ullin Methodist Churches. Melvin "Bucky" Jordan watched the scenes of "Bloody Sunday" on March 7, 1965, in Selma, Alabama, and drove through the night to participate in the second march two days later with Dr. Martin Luther King Jr. Angry people lined the streets and shouted

"N———— lover!" and "You call yourself a preacher!" but he said marching with Dr. King was "truly a life changing experience for me."[2]

The terrorism of the Klan was built on a very real but misplaced fear of all Americans of African descent by many White residents. It was emphasized by a well-defined line that kept people separated based on skin color and encouraged ignorance and an acceptance of stereotypes about any group of people who were not like them. An open and beneficial discussion about the history must begin with an honest and truthful understanding of the past in order to correct the misunderstandings and falsehoods about it. Sometimes that means being reminded of the things we want to forget.

Darrel Dexter
Jonesboro, Illinois
July 23, 2023

Introduction

JOHN A. BEADLES

THE THIRD PRINCIPAL meridian, the main north-south line used in surveying, runs through Pulaski County, Illinois. Indeed, when the cities of Mound City and Mounds combined their high schools, they named the school Meridian. My father, Thomas H. "Tom" Beadles, of Cairo, Illinois, on numerous occasions drove me down what he called "Meridian Road" and told stories about the history of Pulaski County. One was of a "Black soldier" who killed a young woman while robbing her father's store in Villa Ridge in 1924. My father said that the young lady threw a stove lid at the robber and that he shot and killed her. But no documentation has been found to show that the murderer was a soldier; and the victim, Daisy Wilson, did not throw a stove lid at her assailant but attacked him as he was struggling with her father and was shot in the head.

The murder of Daisy Wilson resulted in the attempted lynching of two American men of African descent at Mounds and Mound City, gunfire into the Pulaski County Courthouse, and death by hanging at Mound City of the confessed and convicted murderer. There were 16 documented cases of lynching in the United States in 1924, and Pulaski County came close to adding two more to that number during America's infamous "Age of Lynching" (1880–1940).[1]

In 1924 Pulaski County had a population of approximately 14,700 people.[2] Americans of African descent have consistently comprised about a third of the county's population since the Civil War, and some Black citizens led lives more privileged than those of many other Americans in the 1920s, as a review of prominent Blacks illustrates. Black politicians had long been recognized by the Republican Party in Illinois and were granted patronage.[3] Prominent

4

African American lawyer Charles Leonard Rice was born in 1873 in Pope County but lived in Mound City in Pulaski County until the early 1930s when he moved to Cairo, Illinois. He was a high school graduate who studied law in nearby Vienna, Illinois, under Thomas H. Sheridan and William A. Spann, White lawyers, and was admitted to the bar in 1893. He was also prominent as the city attorney of Mounds from 1895 to 1905 and in 1906 became the first African American master in chancery in Illinois. In 1913 he was appointed to the Illinois State Commerce Commission, which regulates rates and services for public utilities.[4]

Not as active in state politics as Rice, Rome Wellington England was influential in Pulaski County government and was the only American of African descent to have been chairman of a county board in the State of Illinois.[5] He was a native of Paris, Tennessee, and came to Pulaski County about 1907 and was affectionately called "Judge" by many Black and White citizens. A Republican, England served more than 50 years as justice of the peace and over 45 years as county commissioner. A resident of Mounds, the county's second most populous town, England was a successful merchant and made many important connections as a Black Mason and member of Pilgrim Rest Baptist Church.[6]

Another prominent Black man was John Carr Steele, a teacher in Mound City, elected coroner of Pulaski County in 1898. Also a Republican, he continued to serve in that position up to 1921 and was well known in the county. Steele was also a member of the Board of Education in Mound City at the time of his death in 1937.[7] Another prominent educator and farmer was Wren Harris, who won the Republican nomination for county clerk in Pulaski County in 1882. Samuel Patrick Gardner, a teacher and principal at the Ullin "colored school," was born into slavery in 1857 in Weakley County, Tennessee, put on the auction block and sold at the age of four, and came to Mounds with his parents in 1870.[8] Gardner was twice elected county commissioner in Pulaski County.[9] He also taught in a school at Tamms, one near Pulaski, and at Mounds, where among his students was Hugo Chambliss.

Chambliss possessed, built, and rented dwellings (some called them shacks) in Mounds and in Cairo in nearby Alexander County. Most of the Black population in Alexander and Pulaski Counties lived in such housing, making men like Chambliss prosperous. A native of Huntingdon, Tennessee, he was a man with little formal education, but he farmed and ran his real estate business in a prime location on Front Street in Mounds, where his father had operated a grocery and dry goods store.[10] He also served on the Mounds School Board for more than 50 years, was a member of the Meridian School Board, and in the 1960s served on the citizen's advisory committee for Shawnee Community College. He was a 32nd-degree Mason and a member of Pilgrim Rest Baptist Church in Mounds. A Republican precinct committeeman and master in chancery in Pulaski County, he was one of the few Black members of the Cairo Chamber of Commerce.[11] Hugo's father, Haywood Chambliss, was elected a village trustee of Mounds, and his brother, Homer Chambliss, became a physician and lived in Cairo.[12]

Thus, individual local men of African descent could rise to prosperity and have a share of the political power, but most people of color were not so fortunate. Despite the limited progress, there was tension in Pulaski County between Whites and Blacks, although it typically remained under the surface. Karnak, home of one of the county's leading industries, Main Brothers Box Company, was a "sundown town" where Americans of African descent were not allowed to live and were expected to be out of town by sunset if they were working or conducting business there. Thebes, McClure, East Cape Girardeau, and Elco in Alexander County were also known sundown towns, and all the towns that had Black residents were segregated in housing opportunities.

Some 40 years before the incidents focused on in this book, a Black man was lynched in Pulaski County. Nelson Howard of Grand Chain was a section hand on the Wabash Railroad. He had a reputation as a tough, and when county authorities were afraid to approach the drunken and pistol-waving Howard, he was subdued by a huge railroad telegrapher.[13] Howard had killed a White man named John Kane, who also worked for the Wabash Railroad, as an assistant bridge contractor, and had been a steamboat carpenter for years before that. Following the 1883 Independence Day celebration in Cairo, they were returning to Pulaski County on the Wabash excursion train. Both men were still drinking heavily on the train when Howard stumbled into Kane and another White man, who were sitting on the steps of the train's baggage cars as the Wabash was pulling into the Mound City station. They argued and began struggling, and Kane pulled a revolver.[14] Howard fought for the gun and three shots were fired into Kane, who died about an hour later.[15]

Train conductor A. B. Gibson chased Howard, emptying his pistol at the fugitive but missing. Pulaski County Jailer and Deputy Sheriff William Painter and Mound City Marshal Andrew J. Ross assembled a heavily armed posse to go to Grand Chain, where Howard lived. The posse feared a serious confrontation with Howard, who "bore a bad reputation,"[16] but he was arrested without incident and brought to the county jail in Mound City.

On July 6, at about 2 A.M., 75 to 100 masked men surrounded the jail and entered it, confronting Painter and his wife, Anna M. (Kennedy) Painter, and Constable Dille of Villa Ridge, who was on guard duty. Painter refused to open Howard's cell, and Mrs. Painter escaped to raise the alarm. She ran out into the mob in the jail yard yelling for Sheriff Lewis F. Crain but was suddenly stopped and silenced by the men.[17]

The mob leaders demanded that Painter give them the keys to Howard's cell, and when he refused, they produced mauls used for driving railroad spikes and began to batter the cell door. Howard yelled from his cell window to summon help but stopped when the door was opened. Painter, who was being held at gunpoint, said he heard the mob say, "Pick him up boys," and Mrs. Painter heard them say, "Stand up and walk, or we will make you walk." It was at that point that Howard was struck on the head with a spike maul, which crushed his skull and probably killed him. He was also shot three times. Fifty yards from the jail yard gate, his naked body was hung from a tree by a fisherman's trot line.[18]

Four armed Black men had been guarding the Pulaski County jail after Howard's capture, but they did not resist the mob, probably because they were outnumbered. After Howard's body was displayed, Pat Scott, "a colored man with an ear open to trouble," rang the fire bell at the schoolhouse.[19] The determination of one local newspaper was that "there perhaps was some apprehension of the trouble and people generally did not care to mix in it."[20] Sheriff Crain came quickly and cut down Howard's body. The next day's inquest determined that the blow to Howard's head had caused his death and that it had been delivered "at the hands of persons unknown."[21] A $200 reward was offered for information leading to the arrest of members of the lynch mob, which was claimed to be composed of men from outside Mound City.[22]

Following the lynching, Black men thronged the streets of Mound City in protest. Their demonstrations were so vehement that county authorities made numerous attempts to mollify the Black citizens; for their own safety, White railroad men and river men stayed away from Mound City for a considerable period of time.[23] It was a volatile, dangerous town in the days following the lynching.

There were 130 recorded lynchings in the United States in 1883, and Nelson Howard's murder would not seem particularly significant at first glance.[24] This lynching, however, was greatly significant for Pulaski County, especially when contrasted with the attempted lynching in that county in 1924. First, the 1883 mob action gave Pulaski County national attention for the first time since Mound City's prominence as a naval and marine base during the Civil War. Newspapers in St. Louis, Chicago, Nashville, New York City, and elsewhere across the country carried the story and followed it for days.[25] Second, the circumstances following the 1883 lynching showed the power of the county's African American population in contrast to their lack of it 40 years later. Mound City and Pulaski County authorities immediately offered a substantial reward for information leading to the arrest of mob members who had killed Howard.[26] Sheriff Crain was reported to be seeking mobbers forcibly: "A determination exists among the prominent men of Mound City to ferret out the lawless gang at any expense or trouble."[27]

Knowing that convicting lynch mob members would be impossible, the sheriff and "prominent men" broadcast their attitudes to try to placate Black residents of Pulaski County. Within a day of the 1883 lynching, Black men came to Mound City at least three hundred strong. They moved through the streets of town until dark, threatening Whites, including Jailer Painter, City Marshal Ross, and three Wabash Railroad employees, including Conductor Gibson, who had pursued Howard after he killed Kane. Painter, "who was as brave as a lion" and "probably did not know the sensation of fear," and Ross made themselves available to the African Americans and protested that they had done all that they could to prevent the lynching and were now working to bring the perpetrators to justice.[28] Railroad men were the chief suspects in the lynching, and several left Mound City in the days following the lynching; trains on the Wabash road ran "cautiously through Pulaski County for fear that angry negroes moved by a blind thirst for revenge, will tamper with the tracks."[29]

On July 8, 1883, Sheriff Crain, blank arrest warrants in hand, traveled to Cairo, where the Wabash Railroad had many employees, but no arrests were made. The *Cairo Bulletin* declared, "In fact, it would be dangerous to make any arrests now and confine the prisoner anywhere in Pulaski County. The mental state of the colored citizens there is such that they would tear the prisoner limb from limb within twenty-four hours after his confinement."[30]

The Cairo newspaper also claimed White authorities in Pulaski County in 1883 were so concerned that Blacks in the county might physically attack them, as well as railroad men or anyone identified as a suspect, that no legal action was taken. African American physical and political power in Pulaski County was such that they could threaten public officials and ordinary White citizens and be relatively certain that nothing would be done to them legally or otherwise. Slightly more than 40 years later, in 1924, when several Black men were nearly lynched by White mobs, the African American reaction was hardly noted in the press. Indeed, a Black police officer was instrumental in the capture of the African American teenager who was eventually executed for the crime that had catalyzed the lynch mobs.[31]

What had changed with respect to racial relations in Pulaski County between 1883 and 1924? In 1883, the White people accepted and even feared Black power. By 1924, the Ku Klux Klan had arisen to assert White supremacy. Local descendants of southern pioneers were likely to support the tradition of White supremacy promoted by the Ku Klux Klan or were Klansmen themselves. Indeed, there were several Klan klaverns in Pulaski and Alexander Counties by 1924, and some prominent clergymen were Klansmen.[32]

Outside of the Deep South, the national Klan of the 1920s (called the Second Ku Klux Klan) concentrated its activities against Catholics, Jews, and immigrants, but in Pulaski County, perhaps because of the southern origin of most of the White population and the political and economic power of the Black population, the Klan targeted Americans of African descent. This presented a dilemma for Pulaski's Republican officials, some of whom were Klansmen. They needed Black votes to continue their dominance of local government but risked White repudiation if they continued their close relationship with the African American leadership.

There were 60 attempted lynchings in the United States in 1924 and 16 that were successfully carried out.[33] Each of the failed attempts was thwarted in one way or another, but in almost every case it was the local county sheriff and his deputies and supporters who stopped the murder of a suspect or prisoner. In the 1920s, the most widely used means of protecting prisoners from a mob determined to lynch was to move the prisoners to another jurisdiction. If such removal could not be managed, the local sheriff could swear in more deputies who politically or personally supported the sheriff or who were opposed to lynching to the extent that they would risk their lives to stop one. Thus, the sheriff and his deputies had to be prepared to use force to oppose lynch mobs, often composed of their neighbors and acquaintances. The sheriff could also appeal for state help in the form of National Guard troops.[34]

Pulaski County had a challenging cultural divide within its White population in the 1920s. Its original White settlers by and large had been from southern and border states, particularly Kentucky, but some northerners, even New Englanders, had made Pulaski County their home, and Mound City had an unusually northeastern flavor, possessing a rare lower-midwestern Congregational Church.[35] Like in other counties in southern Illinois, "Butternut" and "Yankee" traditions competed for supremacy in popular understanding of what constituted law and, more particularly, order.

Fifteen years previously, in November 1909, what was described as almost the entire White male population of rural Pulaski County had armed themselves and formed their own or joined mobs from bordering Alexander and Union Counties to hunt down Will "Froggy" James, an African American suspect in the rape and murder of a woman living in Cairo. The Alexander County sheriff had custody of James and was trekking through Pulaski County in an effort to board a train to take James to comparative safety elsewhere in Illinois. Sheriff Frank Davis could get no help from Pulaski County residents except for a boy who loaded Davis, a deputy, and James into a wagon at the edge of a swamp and took them to higher ground.[36] Indeed, Karnak Postmaster John D. Copeland was instrumental in keeping mobs informed as to James and his legal captors' possible whereabouts and led one mob himself. He did not hesitate to shatter state law in favor of the then popular notion of nonjudicial justice held by many of his fellow Pulaski County White citizens.

A sizable portion of the Pulaski County population in 1924 believed that it had the sovereign right to lynch African American suspects as mobs surrounded the courthouse in Mound City and fired into it, threatening the lives of deputy sheriffs and Sheriff Ira J. Hudson's wife and son. Why were many Pulaski County people eager to exercise "rough justice" to the point of assaulting county officials and their families, and what role did the Pulaski County Ku Klux Klan have? Why did this unlawful "justice" transform itself into organized, plotted, and planned violence against Americans of African descent?

Historically there had been considerable racial tolerance in Pulaski County. Even after the 1883 lynching, efforts were made by officials to appease an angry Black population. By the 1920s, however, White acceptance of Black Pulaski County had eroded considerably. That decade saw the emergence of the "New Negro," who was prouder and more militant in demanding his rights and now had the legal backing of the National Association for the Advancement of Colored People (NAACP) that had been organized in 1909. The Great Migration brought thousands more African Americans to the North, and clashes between Blacks and Whites called "race riots" broke out in cities nationwide, culminating in the Red Summer of 1919 that saw 38 such riots.[37] The First World War and its aftermath had brought frustrating changes to the United States and to Pulaski County. The prewar way of life had changed, and no doubt many Whites wanted to restore things as they used to be or make their society even more racially exclusive.[38]

The schools in Pulaski County were mostly segregated in 1924, but racial segregation was not particularly rigid when compared to border and southern states and nearby Alexander County. Pulaski County, unlike Alexander County, could not have separate drinking fountains for Whites and Blacks in the courthouse when the chairman of the county commissioners, Rome England, was Black. In Pulaski County there were also African Americans who had more prestige, or at least more economic attainment than most Whites. The fidelity of Republicans in the county to the Grand Old Party was remarkable. The only Pulaski County sheriff in the twentieth century before 1924 who was not a Republican was elected to replace a drunken GOP libertine and was an independent, not a Democrat.[39]

In Pulaski County in 1924 there were the successful and/or assertive Blacks whom the Klan targeted.[40] Many White people in the county must have envied the political and economic success of Black men such as "Judge" England, "Slumlord" Chambliss, and Lawyer Rice. This was the Roaring Twenties, but farm prices had been depressed in rural Pulaski County, as in the rest of the United States, for at least five years. Railroading also was not as profitable as it had been, and river traffic had not increased enough to revive Mound City to near its heyday in the early 1900s. Chicago, the epitome of a 1920s American city, was less than a day's train trip away, and the sons and daughters of leading families were going there and elsewhere to make better or more interesting lives for themselves.[41]

White people in Pulaski County faced all the common stresses of 1920s America—rural stagnation, transportation evolution, and loss of promising young people to cities—plus the reality of a Black population that possessed economic and political power considerably above the American norm. Black people in Pulaski County lived among Whites in substantial numbers; indeed, they made up about a third of the county's population, but they did not fit into the ideal racial relationship according to some Whites. That is, Pulaski County Black people had not been backed into a clearly defined subservient, economic, cultural, and political station.[42]

In the early 1920s, many White people in Pulaski County felt they had reasons for putting Black people in what they considered to be "their place." When many Whites asked themselves what the instrument was for doing so, the answer was the Ku Klux Klan. It swept through Pulaski and Alexander Counties like a storm. The KKK bloc recruited in southern Illinois, as they did elsewhere, targeting fraternal organizations and Protestant churches, ensuring that many Klan members would be embedded in social networks and actively involved in the life of the county.[43] In 1920s America, there was an everyday, ordinary quality to the Klan's presence in the dominant White, Protestant America. Klan membership in many communities was an open secret and included public officials, White Protestant ministers, and ordinary and prominent citizens alike.[44]

If the Klan could be the instrument for a more rigorous White supremacy in Pulaski County in the early 1920s, what could be the means for more absolute White subordination of Black people? Not far away in bordering Alexander County was an answer. Cairo and Alexander County between 1910 and 1914 experienced political and structural changes that ensured White supremacy over the local African Americans would become increasingly pronounced, while Black hopes of racial equality would be progressively diminished and delayed for decades.

A coalition of White and Black Republicans, then still the party of Lincoln and Black citizenship, dominated county politics in the late nineteenth and early twentieth centuries in Alexander County. While not as Republican as Pulaski County itself, the Alexander GOP was winning most county offices by 1900.[45] This political shift had resulted because of patronage for African Americans. There were Black sheriff's deputies and justices of the peace in Alexander County. Black people also had influence in determining White political candidacy.[46]

The catalyst that changed the situation in Alexander County was an attempted lynching in 1910 in Cairo in which Black deputies defended a Black prisoner and a prominent White man in the lynch mob was killed. Daily newspapers increasingly blamed the locality's Black people for the troubles and called for greater control over them by political and social changes.[47] Some White Republicans thought the party was too cozy and comfortable with the county's and city's Black populations.[48] This started the effort to change politics and society in Alexander County by electing Democrats to county offices, especially in law enforcement positions, such as sheriff and state's attorney.[49]

The November 1910 elections saw Democratic Sheriff Alexander Fraser chosen in something of a landslide.[50] The new sheriff broadcast that county politics was now going to be dominated by Whites. Indeed, Illinois's leading newspaper, the *Chicago Tribune*, in discussing Alexander County's new "White man's government," quoted the county's new Democratic sheriff as saying that under his administration the only Black people found in the courthouse would be behind bars.[51] Both the *Tribune* and Carbondale's *Daily Free Press* stated that Black people would no longer be a factor in Alexander County politics.[52] Fraser's election as sheriff signaled a triumph of White supremacy in Alexander County, as all African American deputy sheriffs were fired, the county jail was segregated, and racially separate water fountains and toilets were established in county buildings.[53]

Black political power in Cairo was further reduced in 1913. By a two-to-one vote, Cairo citizens threw out aldermanic government and adopted a city commission. All the commissioners would be elected at large, which meant that no Black commissioners would be elected until the 1970s, when a civil rights lawsuit created a "safe" Black seat on the city council.[54] Thus, political devices still used to the present day in other places to disenfranchise American minorities, such as at-large voting and rigid registration, were now in place in Alexander County and Cairo.

Many White supremacists in neighboring Pulaski County in 1924 envied how Alexander County and Cairo had suppressed the political power of African Americans. They recognized also that violence had played a role in Alexander County's transformation from a barely segregated to a rigidly segregated county. In Pulaski County White and Black Republicans were still too cozy and comfortable with each other for some tastes, especially among the Klansmen, who were growing in number and influence in 1924. What was to be done to make Pulaski County more segregated, more under White political and social control like Alexander County? The county commissioners were already elected at-large, and there was still always one Black commissioner. The sizable local African American minority still had a significant role in the Republican Party. In Alexander County from 1909 to 1914, when social supports for an integrated city and county were crumbling and a biracial political structure was in the process of collapse, violence in the form of lynching and attempted lynching was the first step leading to racial segregation and suppression.[55]

Might a lynching in Pulaski County cow the social and political pretensions of Black Pulaski County and serve notice that Pulaski, like nearby Alexander, was governed and controlled by White men? In 1924, a lynching was attempted in Pulaski County. In 1925, a Black man was legally executed by hanging in Mound City, the county seat. The White and Black Republican coalition, however, still was not broken in those years and would strongly endure.[56]

Pulaski White lynchers were aroused in 1924, and the Ku Klux Klan and its rhetoric had encouraged and empowered them. The third of the population that was Black made no public demonstration of their opposition and either remained silent or were silenced by the local media, which did not publicize the African American assessment of the terrible events of 1924.[57] So perhaps the attempted lynching in 1924 and public hanging of 1925 had something of that desired effect. Black Pulaski County men were not publicly expressing their anger in 1924 or 1925 as they had done with the 1883 lynching at Mound City. Were they now going to the back doors of Republican leaders and newspapers to quietly ask for their share of what political benefits existed, as was the custom in Alexander County at the time?

No Alexander County Black Republicans were elected to office even after the party returned to power in 1920, but some were appointed as deputy sheriffs and marshals in the county, as they were in Pulaski County. This type of political patronage was necessary to the success of the Republican Party in the two counties. Efficient law enforcement there also depended on having lawmen who were Black and White. In 1924, while the National Guard troops held back a mob bent on lynching two Black suspects in Mound City, an

African American lawman subdued the killer of Daisy Wilson, and another Black officer got his accomplice to confess to the crime.[58]

Racial cooperation was successful in the area of Republican politics and law enforcement but not in other sectors like education, religion, and society at large. Many White residents clung to the idea of White supremacy and consciously or otherwise taught it to their children. This sentiment deterred and limited progress in the region for generations, even after it was used as the foundation on which to build the Second Ku Klux Klan.

CHAPTER ONE

The Mythical Klan and Rumors
of Its Second Coming

THE SECOND WAVE of the Ku Klux Klan swept into Pulaski and Alexander Counties in the 1920s as it spread across the state and country. For decades before, a foundation of half-truths about the Klan were peddled to the public, and that laid the foundation for the reemergence of the Klan. A mythical version of the original Ku Klux Klan was offered to the people through pseudohistorical novels and the entertainment medium of stage. Romantic plays and books about the First Ku Klux Klan of the previous century conditioned the people to accept a positive view of the Klan. When it came time to revive an official Ku Klux Klan organization, the foundation had been laid.

The drama *The Ku Klux Klan* was first performed at the Cairo Opera House on April 21, 1906. The two-column advertisement in one of the newspapers, the *Cairo Evening Citizen*, showed a revised illustration from the first edition of the book *The Clansman* by the Reverend Thomas F. Dixon Jr., on which the play was loosely based. The picture showed a hooded member on a white horse, with the flaming crosses used in the original replaced by the letters KKK. This is "a drama of absorbing interest dealing with the 'Invisible Empire,' which in 1870 stamped out Negro Rule in the South," the advertisement promised.[1] Advance tickets ranging in price from twenty-five cents to a dollar went on sale April 20 at the Opera House Box Office for matinee and evening performances. Every ticket was sold in less than 24 hours.

The *Cairo Bulletin* stated that "no play presented within the last decade has been viewed with greater interest or with more favor than the 'Ku Klux Klan.'"[2] The enthusiastic reception of the play was a sign that the time was ripe for a rebirth of the Ku Klux Klan, which had mostly disappeared by the late 1870s, but the racism on which it was founded had not diminished, and the organization was waiting for the right moment to re-emerge in the form of the Second Ku Klux Klan. The role Dixon was to play in the restoration of the Ku Klux Klan was to whitewash the Klan's image as one of a violent terrorist organization and recast it as the onetime heroic savior of White man's rule and defender of White womanhood. A growing perception among many White citizens by the early 1900s was that they were losing their grip on power and that violent African Americans and other groups, such as new immigrants and Jews, were a rising threat to their way of life and to White supremacy and White womanhood.

Dixon was well known in Cairo, and after publishing *The Leopard's Spots,* his first novel in the Ku Klux Klan trilogy, he lectured on February 3, 1904, at the Cairo Opera House, two years before his play arrived in town.[3] His lecture was titled "Backbone" and was sponsored by the Cairo Women's Club, the Young Men's Christian Association (YMCA), and the Cairo High School Library Association.[4] He obviously had the attention of many White leaders in Cairo and would soon gain their approval if he did not already have it. The *Cairo Bulletin* stated Dixon would "present his convictions on the race problem without fear or partiality."[5] The city's daily morning newspaper stated Dixon "looks awkward when you first see him . . . and looks more awkward as he grasps his thin chin in his long bony hand and peers at the people before him. But when he begins to talk and move in concert with his sentences, you remember only that he is giving a most brilliant display of vocal fireworks."[6] Dixon spoke for an hour and a half and "no platform speaker who has been heard in Cairo ever made a deeper or more satisfactory impression on his audience."[7] The people in the White audience liked what they heard and seemed in agreement with Dixon's message of White supremacy.

Dixon's portrayal of a heroic Ku Klux Klan was readily accepted in southern Illinois. One of his plays was billed in Cairo as "a direct contradiction of *Uncle Tom's Cabin*," which had been performed numerous times over the decades in Cairo and at "opera houses" in nearby towns like Anna, Mound City, Tamms, and Ullin.[8] *Uncle Tom's Cabin* by Harriet Beecher Stowe was published in 1852 and influenced public opinion against slavery, at least in the North, by portraying the evils and violence inherent in the institution and by humanizing those enslaved. Dixon, a former Baptist preacher, attended a theatrical performance of *Uncle Tom's Cabin* in 1901 and left so offended by the sympathetic portrayal of Black characters and the villainous characterization of White southern slaveholders that he vowed to write a book to, in his view, set the record straight.[9] His book was *The Leopard's Spots: A Romance of the White Man's Burden—1865–1900* published in 1902.

Dixon was overtly racist and his purpose was to spread White supremacy across the country, north and south. He capitalized on the "black threat," the fear instilled in many White citizens of Americans of African descent, especially Black men, which was largely encouraged by the press, including southern Illinois newspapers. Dixon wrote, "Over all the earth hung the shadow of the freed Negro, transformed by the exigency of war from a Chattel to be bought and sold into a possible Beast to be feared and guarded."[10] Dixon borrowed the villain Simon Legree, the murderer of Uncle Tom from the pages of *Uncle Tom's Cabin*, and made him the villain in his book. Dixon's Legree was cowardly, had sold those he enslaved as rumors of the Civil War started, and then disguised himself as a woman for several years to avoid service in either army. After the war, Legree became a scalawag (White southern Republican) and rose to the position of North Carolina speaker of the house. Legree worked to organize freedmen (former enslaved persons) into Union leagues to take the land from the White men and make them the servants of Americans of African descent. In one scene, a company of Black soldiers surrounded the house of Tom Camp, a poor White man who had lost a leg in the war fighting for the Confederacy; kidnapped Annie, Camp's 16-year-old daughter; and carried her screaming to the woods. The White men in the house, following Camp's orders, shot as the soldiers were fleeing and hit Annie in the temple, killing her. When her lifeless body was brought back to the house and laid on her bed, Tom exclaimed, "Don't, don't cry so! It might have been worse. Let us thank God she was saved from them brutes."[11] This event was treated like the trumpet of God that "called the sleeping manhood of the Anglo-Saxon race to life again," and the Ku Klux Klan was created in this romantic fictional account. The White cavalry rode across the countryside and "every negro found guilty of a misdemeanor was promptly thrashed and warned against its recurrence."[12] Charlie Gaston, another character, makes a rousing speech in which he declares, "This is a white man's government, conceived by white men, and maintained by white men through every year of its history—and by the God of our Fathers it shall be ruled by white men until the Arch-angel shall call the end of time!"[13]

Dixon's work of fiction was a blockbuster, selling 200,000 copies the first year. The reception of his novel was encouragement enough for him to follow it with *The Clansman: An Historical Romance of the Ku Klux Klan* in 1905, which Dixon dedicated to "my uncle, Colonel Leroy McAfee, Grand Titan of the Invisible Empire Ku Klux Klan."[14] This second book was the most popular and best known of Dixon's trilogy about his mythical Ku Klux Klan, which concluded with the third volume, *The Traitor: A Story of the Fall of the Invisible Empire*, in 1907.

The Clansman opens with the story of Ben Cameron, a 19-year-old Confederate soldier under arrest and sentenced to be shot. President Lincoln, who is portrayed as a southern gentleman sympathetic to the plight of White southerners and opposed to the "Africanization" of the South, pardons the young soldier. Cameron, in this fictional account, goes on to become the grand dragon of the South Carolina Ku Klux Klan. The villain of the second novel is Augustus Caesar, or "Gus," who was formerly enslaved by the Cameron family but was told, "As a sovereign voter, you, once their slave, are not only their equal—you are their master."[15] Gus, captain of the Negro League, and three of his men rape Marion Lenoir, the childhood sweetheart of Cameron, while her mother is bound and helpless. Afterward the women, in their shame, decide to burn their clothes, hide any other evidence of the crime, and commit suicide by throwing themselves from Lover's Leap, hoping people will think they fell to their deaths accidentally and the rape will remain a secret. Gus is captured by the Klan, gives a confession after being hypnotized, and is lynched. His body is placed where it will be found, and pinned to his shirt as a warning, written in red ink, is "K. K. K." The message throughout the books was clear—Americans of African descent, especially Black men, were the enemy who must be guarded against by a White army, the Ku Klux Klan, in order to protect White America, especially White women.

Dixon wrote, "For a thick-lipped, flat-nosed, spindle-shanked negro, excluding his nauseating animal odour, to shout in derision over the hearths and homes of White men and women is an atrocity too monstrous for belief. Our people are yet dazed by its horror."[16] Civilization must be saved from this "barbarism" of African American suffrage and Black rule, he argued. In the book, the Klan issued orders that all Americans of African descent were to surrender their guns and disband the "Negro Militia." The last line of the novel concludes, "Civilization has been saved, and the South redeemed from shame."[17]

His last novel of the Klan trilogy, *The Traitor*, is set in North Carolina from 1870 to 1872 and centers on the fictional grand dragon of the state's Klan, John

Graham, and his enemy, Republican Judge Hugh Butler, who orders the arrest of all Klansmen. Graham follows the orders of Nathan Bedford Forrest, the grand wizard, and instructs his men to burn their hoods and robes, bury the ashes, and take their final march. Graham tells his men, "Boys, I thank you. Our work is done. We have rescued our state from Negro rule."[18] Another character reorganizes a group within two weeks, using the Klan's name and costume, and begins terrorizing the countryside, trying to regulate the lives and morals of both Blacks and Whites and, as Graham claimed, "disgracing the uniform of the Ku Klux Klan."[19] Enemies of the Klan dress up in their robes and hoods and assassinate Judge Butler, which in Dixon's fictional story is what led to passage of the Enforcement Act of 1870, which prohibited bands from meeting in disguise in public in order to violate other citizens' constitutional rights. Klan members are arrested and Graham is wrongfully accused of killing Judge Butler. At his trial in federal court, the jury is composed of "one dirty, ignorant white scalawag and eleven coal-black Negroes."[20] A Black "sanctified" preacher, Isaac A. Postle, falsely testifies he saw Graham stab and kill Butler but is forced to recant. The jury sentences Graham to five years in a federal prison, but he is pardoned.

Dixon's novels were not historically accurate in their portrayal of the Klan, but the myth began to be accepted as the truth about the origins of the Klan by many Whites. The misinformation about the Klan that Dixon casually disseminated is what made his books such dangerous tools in the hands of those fighting to maintain and, in a few places, reinstitute White supremacy. The image of the Ku Klux Klan was erroneously revised from a violent organization of the Reconstruction Era that terrorized Americans of African descent and some Whites; it became a heroic one that had redeemed the South from a corrupt and incompetent government by Black men and, of course, protected and avenged the virtue of White womanhood. The novels were read by millions and spawned several plays that were performed by traveling entertainers in vaudeville houses across the country, such as the one in Cairo.

Not everyone was fooled by Dixon's portrayal of the Klan, and many were displeased by the success of the dramas. Nationally, in every city where the play The Ku Klux Klan or a later version, The Clansman, was performed, there was vocal opposition. On the day before the performance of The Ku Klux Klan at the opera house in Cairo in 1906, the Cairo Bulletin stated that there was "some talk that negroes will try to prevent presentation of this sensational play."[21] "Colored" citizens of the town made a formal protest to the manager of the Cairo Opera House, but the play went on as scheduled. The play was set in 1868 in Tennessee, when, the newspaper alleged, "carpetbaggers organized negroes into loyal leagues and other secret political societies and fed their deluded followers on promises of social equality and supremacy over the whites." To confront this situation, "the white men of the South organized the 'Invisible Empire' more popularly known as the Ku Klux Klan, a secret order, to overthrow carpetbag rule and negro domination."[22] The play promised to stir the emotions of the audience "to an almost uncontrollable pitch." If there were demonstrations outside the opera house, they were not reported in the press. The only concern reported in the newspaper was that some theatergoers were "compelled to pay excessive prices to speculators for choice locations."[23]

The Cairo Opera House attracted mostly members of the White business and professional classes in Cairo, but no doubt there were others in attendance from neighboring towns in Pulaski and Alexander Counties. In addition, there were more than half a dozen railroads, most importantly the Illinois Central, which brought passengers and freight into and through Cairo from across southern Illinois, the tristate region, and beyond.[24] Many White citizens in the area received the performance of *The Ku Klux Klan* with enthusiasm as a celebration of White supremacy, and across the country such performances embittered feelings against Americans of African descent. The narrative of the Klan as the redeemers of White America was being planted in the minds of many as the true story of Reconstruction, if it was not there already. Dixon's trilogy provided great propaganda for White supremacists.

Interest in Dixon's mythical Klan continued to grow among White citizens in southern Illinois after the initial show on April 21, 1906, at the Cairo Opera House. Later, on April 4, 1907, Ferris's Comedians again performed the play *The Ku Klux Klan*. The *Cairo Evening Citizen* this time called it "a play along the same lines as 'The Clansman' dealing with the same theme which is at present hour the great question which confronts American people."[25] The question seemed to be: what is the "place" of Americans of African descent in American society? The *Cairo Bulletin* called *The Ku Klux Klan* a companion piece to *The Clansman*, which had been banned in many cities for inciting racial hatred and presenting "the race question in a more startling manner."[26] Prices were ten cents and twenty-five cents per ticket, depending on seating.

A production of the better known and more notorious play *The Clansman*, written by Dixon himself and based on his novel of the same name, was performed one night only at the Cairo Opera House on January 21, 1907.[27] The *Cairo Evening Citizen* claimed the play was set in a time when "carpet-baggers and upstart negroes seized the reins of government." The *Cairo Bulletin* stated that the play "pictures the days when courage, self-sacrifice and chivalric deeds removed the fetters that held the southern [White] people in bondage."[28] The prices for tickets were $1.50 for seating on the entire lower floor and 50 cents for the gallery, more than those for *The Ku Klux Klan*. It was an unusually elaborate production. Three Pullman sleeper cars and two baggage cars on a special Illinois Central train were arranged to bring the cast of 40, the elaborate scenery, and "five specially trained horses" to Cairo for the performance. The play once again entertained a sold-out audience, "crowded from pit to dome."[29] The *Cairo Bulletin* stated that it was the largest crowd ever seen at the opera house and that the audience was mostly composed of southern sympathizers.[30]

Just as in other larger cities, resistance to the performance of *The Clansman* was again quickly organized in Cairo.[31] There were many reasons to protest the play. African American characters were portrayed by White actors in blackface, which a modern audience would find offensive. This was not the chief offense recognized by playgoers of the early 1900s, as minstrel shows had appeared in Cairo and almost all southern Illinois towns with no great outcry, and local citizens put on their own minstrel performances for local audiences.[32] Earlier minstrel shows had always portrayed Blacks as unintelligent, comical, and a lazy class of people who were more prone to sing and dance than to work.[33] *The Clansman* was different than the routine forms of racist entertainment many Americans of African descent had grown accustomed to tolerating and marked a leap backward in race relations.

The Clansman did not just make Americans of African descent the butt of jokes to be laughed at and ridiculed, but the play and the novel it was based on portrayed them as the enemies of White America and civilization itself. Black men were depicted as lascivious and unable to control their lustful desires, and were to be feared and must be controlled by White men in order to protect the purity of White womanhood. All of Dixon's books and the plays based on them portrayed American men of African descent in one of three ways: They were crafty and scheming, finding ways to insult and seek revenge on their former enslavers; a few were portrayed as naively accepting White supremacy, remaining loyal and submissive to their former masters; and others were corrupt or ignorant tools easily manipulated by White northern Republicans and Black leaders.

A meeting of leading Black citizens was called at Twelfth Street Baptist Church in Cairo to discuss the showing of *The Clansman*, and after deliberation, resolutions were adopted that stated Dixon was "the worst enemy of the negro race." A committee of African American citizens was formed and met with Mayor George Parsons and Chief of Police Martin S. Egan to ask them to prevent the play from being performed, but the two officials claimed it was not in their power to ban the play. The committee then requested that the "objectionable" features be removed from the performance, but that was also refused. The play was banned by mayors in some cities, including Philadelphia; Montgomery, Alabama; and Macon, Georgia, but not in Cairo.[34]

The manager of the Cairo Opera House, Daniel Lewis Williamson, a young White Cairo native, also met with the committee and tried to convince them that there was "nothing in the play to injure the negro race" and that they were being misled by outside agitators who were trying to "start something." He claimed there was nothing in the play to which "intelligent negroes" could object any more than White people could object to productions of *Uncle Tom's Cabin*.[35] It is likely that Williamson had seen the play and observed its blatant racism, but like many other White Americans, he felt that White supremacy was not harmful to Americans of African descent and in fact was in their best interest. Perhaps he saw banning of some works while allowing others as a slippery slope toward even more censorship, or maybe he just did not want to lose the chance to profit financially from a sold-out audience.

A writer for the *Cairo Bulletin* believed that Dixon wrote *The Clansman* just to "lure the dollars from the pockets of the people" and stated that "it is hardly applicable to present conditions anywhere, except as they may be reflected in a few overheated minds from time to time." He wrote after the performance, "The Clansman has come and gone, and all is serene. . . . The little ripple stirred up by a few negro citizens some days ago with their protests against its production had lost itself in the broad expanse of public good feeling or indifference before the play came, and while the play had a full house, it caused but little stir." As is often the case when publicity hype builds up lofty expectations, "many people who saw it were disappointed."[36]

Racist feelings toward Americans of African descent were present in southern Illinois before the appearance of Dixon's books and play, but his works encouraged those positions and gave credence to them. Dixon applauded and celebrated lynching and violence against African Americans in his books and play, which were known to some southern Illinoisans. The opinions of Archdeacon Edward L. Roland, rector of the Church of the Redeemer in Cairo, fell closely in line with those of Dixon when he spoke at a synod of the Episcopal Church in Springfield, Illinois, on December 5, 1905. He exhorted that missionary work among the "negroes of Cairo" was needed, as they "were as a class about the worst negroes in any city in the Union, being responsible for the large majority of the crimes committed in the city."[37] Roland even went as far as to say a mistake had been made in giving Black men suffrage.

In September 1907, Calvary Baptist Church in Cairo held a tent revival meeting attended by over a thousand citizens from the area and was the largest series of meetings ever held in the town. The revival was organized by the Reverend Dr. Liston D. Bass, pastor of the church, and the huge tent was set up at Twenty-Eighth and Sycamore Streets.[38] The evangelist was the nationally known Dr. Henry Marvin Wharton, author of *White Blood: A Story of the South*, which the *Cairo Bulletin* called "a novel about supremacy of White blood and the unconquerable future of the Saxon race."[39] The book was similar to those written by Dixon and created interest beyond the religious message that Rev. Wharton delivered. Dixon had become the best-known promoter of White supremacy in the nation, but they could also be found elsewhere, locally and nationally.

Local newspapers in Alexander and Pulaski Counties in the first decades of the twentieth century created or enforced their White readers' racist fear of African Americans, who were always presented as the "others." Their sensational media accounts kept many White and Black people on edge. A sampling of front-page local headlines from the 1905 *Cairo Bulletin* includes these: "Police Capture a Negro Murderer,"[40] "Dying Negress and White Youth Had a Suicide Compact,"[41] "New Evidence Found against the Negro,"[42] "Illinois Central Flagman Killed by Negro,"[43] "Negro Burglar Shot Down by Ullin Storekeeper,"[44] "Wade Hampton Probably Fatally Wounded by Two Negroes,"[45] "Negroes Who Make Business of Peddling Cocaine Are Fined,"[46] "Slashed His Neck—Cairo's New Pitcher Victim of Negro's Assault—Was Walking Downtown with Friends When Negro Stuck Knife in His Throat,"[47] "Killed by a Negro—Shot Down Trying to Arrest a Black Bandit,"[48] "Jim Caruthers Perhaps Fatally Cut by Negro,"[49] "Negro Assaulted Young White Girl,"[50] "Was Shot by Negroes,"[51] "Negro Held for Woman's

Murder,"[52] "Darky Who Shot at Darky and Killed White Man Given Light Sentence,"[53] "Negro Held for Murder of White Man,"[54] "Young Lady Attacked on Prominent Street by Black Highwayman,"[55] "Negroes of Cairo Are the Worst of Any City in the Union,"[56] "Brave Teacher Kills a Negro,"[57] "Mob Formed to Hang Negro Who Killed White Man,"[58] and "Negro Kills Himself to Escape Lynching."[59] Similar headlines can be found in southern Illinois newspapers for any year through the 1920s.

Consciously or unconsciously, such headlines connected the word "negro" with crime and fear in the minds of White readers. When a Black man or woman committed a crime, it was not just the individual who was subject to judgment, but all Black people were made to pay. This was not the same for White society. It was obvious that there were violent crimes committed by Black citizens, but there were also just as atrocious crimes perpetrated by White men and women. When Whites committed crimes against Black citizens or other Whites, their race was not blasted in the headlines to create a fear of all White men. Americans of African descent did not receive the same fair treatment by the local or national media in the early 1900s.

The racist sentiment that was sweeping much of the country in the first decades of the twentieth century also plainly manifested itself in southern Illinois. Thebes, a small town along the Mississippi River in Alexander County, was the site of "race trouble" in July 1900. The village had no Black residents, but when "some colored men" were brought to Thebes to load lumber from a river barge into a railroad car, trouble erupted. The workers, who were told that they could not stay in town and that they had to leave by 4 P.M., became frightened and left.[60] No Americans of African descent were allowed to live or work in Thebes until construction of the Thebes Bridge across the Mississippi River began in 1903, and White resentment toward their presence led to a race riot in the town and culminated in the lynching of one African American teenager and the shooting of several other Black workers.[61]

In Cairo, a group identified in the press as "White Caps" made a night raid on the house of Mary C. Bettis, a "negress" living on Thirty-Fourth Street, on July 7, 1907.[62] "White Caps," sometimes called "White Cappers," were disguised vigilante gangs that operated outside the law. They kicked in the front door of Bettis's house, broke several windows, and stormed into her home. Bettis made a complaint before the grand jury in Cairo and even identified some of the men, but the jury chose not to indict them.[63] Bettis was a widow and formerly a school teacher who lived with her mother-in-law, Ada-line Bettis, and her 20-year-old daughter, Jessie A. Bettis.[64] Bettis told the grand jury that the men were "indignant citizens of the neighborhood" who attacked her house because she allowed a White man to stay there. The news-paper did not identify the White man but stated he was forced to make a dash out the door and through a pond to escape. Another witness stated that the man living there had built and furnished the house for Bettis and that "they lived in an almost open state of adultery." The *Cairo Bulletin* reported that the grand jury was "much more inclined to find bills [of indictment] against the woman and her shameless white paramour" than the "White Caps," and their crime went unpunished.[65]

Not all racism took a violent turn. In Mound City, White citizens donated funds to create Oak Park on public ground around the courthouse square in July 1907. The park was for Whites only, and when members of a church in Mound City petitioned the Pulaski County commissioners to also allow them entrance to the park, the park commissioners took drastic action. The "col-ored brethren" were told the park would be divided and that American citi-zens of African descent would be responsible for the expenses and work of improving their part of the park. The offer of a separate park was refused, and the park commissioners closed the park rather than open it to everyone and wrote a sarcastic letter to the county commissioners extending their "cor-dial thanks" for the use of the courthouse square as a park "for the season of two weeks."[66] The African American community in Mound City was at least briefly awakened and becoming politically active in a way not found elsewhere in the region.

In nearby Johnson County, the appearance of night riders was first noted in May 1908.[67] African American families moved from Kentucky in the early spring of 1908 to Vienna in Johnson County and found jobs working for farmers southeast of town. The families and their employers received no-tices that the Black workers had to leave, but the warnings were ignored. On the night of May 23, 1908, a home occupied by one of the families living on the William P. Walker farm was riddled with bullets and shots. Another Black family living on the farm of Justus W. Shinn was visited in a similar manner.

The novels of Dixon and their performances in theaters did not make a majority of White southern Illinoisans or those in the rest of the country racist, but the popularity and enthusiastic acceptance of his books, plays, and films are evidence of just how racist the country already was soon after the turn of the century. Historians call that time period the nadir, or lowest point, of race relations in the United States.[68] Dixon's works contradict what many knew to be the truth of the origins of the Ku Klux Klan and the reign of terror that the group introduced during the Reconstruction Era. What Dixon's and similar books and plays by other writers did was dramatically transform and whitewash the image of the Klan and lay the groundwork for the coming of the Second Ku Klux Klan, which would make its appearance in southern Illinois in the early 1920s.

CHAPTER TWO

Memories of the First Klan

T HE PEOPLE OF SOUTHERN ILLINOIS, White and Black, should have known that the mythical Klan portrayed in Dixon's trilogy was not the historical Ku Klux Klan that they remembered or had heard their parents and grandparents talk about. Many Americans of African descent, especially in Cairo, Mound City, Mounds, and Ullin, came to southern Illinois as freedmen after the Civil War, and some fled Klan violence in the South during the Reconstruction Era. There also were several gangs of men in southern Illinois being called the Ku Klux Klan that were highly active as vigilante groups from 1872 to 1876. Almost all of the press in the region at that time were virulently against the southern Illinois Klan. Editorial after editorial was written against the Klan when violence was directed against Whites, and, just as predictably, editorials denied the existence of the Klan in the South or in southern Illinois when violence was directed toward Blacks. The genuine Ku Klux Klan had different origins than the mythical one portrayed by Thomas Dixon Jr. in his trilogy romanticizing the Klan. It also was a different version of the southern Ku Klux Klan that appeared in some southern Illinois counties during Reconstruction, the 12-year period following the Civil War.

What is called by historians the First Ku Klux Klan was organized in December 1865 in Pulaski, Giles County, Tennessee, by a half dozen former Confederate soldiers as a secret fraternal society; it spread as it evolved throughout the South.[1] In 1867, the different branches of the Klan met and united to form "The Invisible Empire of the South." The social goal of the First Ku Klux Klan was to reimpose servitude on Americans of African descent, and its main political goal was to disfranchise Black voters and thereby disempower them. Thus, the aim of the Klan was to reinforce and preserve White supremacy over African Americans. Former Confederate General

Nathan Bedford Forrest joined the Klan in 1867 and became its first grand wizard. When asked during a Congressional inquiry in 1871 why the Klan had been formed, Forrest replied it was organized out of fear. He said, "The negroes were holding night meetings; were going about; were becoming insolent. . . . Ladies were ravished by some of those negroes. . . . There was a great deal of insecurity."[2]

The Klan was also a backlash from White southern Democrats, most of them ex-Confederates, against Radical Republicans who controlled Congress after the Civil War. Republicans made great advancements toward social and political equality for Black and White Americans during Reconstruction. In 1868 they were able to pass the Fourteenth Amendment, which said everyone born in the United States, including anyone who had been previously enslaved, was a citizen and guaranteed all citizens equal protection under the law. Two years later they achieved ratification of the Fifteenth Amendment, which gave all male citizens, including those who were formerly enslaved, the right to vote. In many places of the South, until the Amnesty Act of 1872 restored to former Confederates the right to vote and hold office, Americans of African descent formed the majority of the electorate and were successful in electing Black officeholders for the first time. In 1875 Congress enacted the Civil Rights Act, which prohibited racial discrimination in accommodations in public transportation, hotels, and restaurants, and it was the law of the land until 1883, when it was ruled unconstitutional.

Southern Democrats campaigned against what they called the Africanization of the South, and the Klan began using racial terror—lynching and other brutal acts against African American voters and some White Republicans to keep them from the polls by threats and intimidation. Black churches and schools were targeted for burning. The Klan wanted what they called "Redemption," the return to power of the same White, southern Democrats who had ruled before the Civil War. After a year as grand wizard, Forrest called for the disbandment of the Klan and the destruction of members' robes and hoods because he thought the out-of-control violence was hurting the achievement of the Klan's goals of White-only rule. Only a few local chapters followed his order, however, and the Ku Klux Klan continued without his leadership, and so did the violence.

The Congressional response was to pass the Enforcement Acts, which included the Ku Klux Klan Act of 1871, intended to protect freedmen's civil rights, especially voting rights in the South, and to crush Klan violence. The

Ku Klux Klan Act made it a crime to deprive any citizen of his rights, privileges, or immunities secured by the Constitution and laws. The act, signed into law by President Ulysses S. Grant, was successful in dismantling the First Ku Klux Klan in the South but only after its goal of disfranchising Americans of African descent was already achieved in most of the region.

The Amnesty Act of 1872 helped restore White rule by restoring the right to vote and hold public office to most former Confederates. One by one, despite the prosecution of some Klansmen, the states in the old Confederacy returned to all-White home rule, and some Americans of African descent returned to a second slavery or at least a less-than-second-class citizenship. By 1876, northern Republican support for Reconstruction waned; federal troops, which had protected Black voters, were pulled from the southern military districts; and one by one southern state governments "redeemed" the South: by the first decade of the 1900s, the Constitutional right to vote had been diluted by state governments issuing literacy tests, grandfather clauses, poll taxes, White primaries, and violent intimidation to the point that few African Americans were allowed to vote in the South. Control was back in the hands of former Confederates and other like-minded Whites and would remain so even a century later. The political goal of the Klan had been achieved by White Democrats in the South with the help of indifferent White Republicans in the North, who thought it was more important to unite White America than to protect the rights of Black America.

Not only was the Ku Klux Klan active in the South, but also some southern Illinois counties achieved notoriety during the decade following the Civil War for what was called Klan activity. In March 1868, the *Cairo Democrat* reported on rumors of a local Ku Klux Klan in Alexander County, and in July a settlement of Americans of African descent (the newspaper writer snidely called them "cullud pussons") just outside of Cairo on the Mississippi River claimed that they were visited by the night-riding Ku Klux Klan.[3] According to the reports, "All the white carpet-baggers were notified by the negroes of a Ku-Klux invasion," and each night "ten negroes and four white 'scalawags' stood guard armed with guns." About one hundred men, all on black horses, rode through the settlement but disappeared when shots were fired. The newspaper seems to have exaggerated the report in order to cast a general disbelief that the "mythical" Klan was active in Alexander County. In fact, newspaper editor John H. Oberly tried to convince his readers of the lie that reports of a night-riding Ku Klux Klan anywhere in the South were only fables promulgated by frightened, superstitious "negroes" and White Republican leaders in order to continue military rule in the South.

A couple of months later, a fugitive from the Klan in Tennessee and a former member of the Invisible Empire convinced some citizens of Mound City in Pulaski County that there was a Ku Klux Klan chapter of about 80 members there, which he said was headed by Romeo Friganza, a joiner at the shipyard, a Democrat, and a native of Spain.[4] Friganza denied membership in the Klan, and when he tried to locate his accuser to confront him, he found that he had fled the county. The Cairo newspaper debunked the report as "another of those absurd Ku-Klux stories." The *Cairo Bulletin* went as far as to say that there was no such organization as the Ku Klux Klan anywhere in the North or South "except in the minds of superstitious negroes and carpetbaggers who have been inciting them [African Americans] to deeds of violence against the disfranchised (White) men of the South."[5] Oberly thus absurdly suggested that the only Klan-related violence in the South was directed by anti-Klan advocates against unfortunate White disfranchised ex-Confederates.

A few years later, in Alexander County, a group calling itself "KKK" again appeared in the local news. In June 1874, it was reported that "Ku Klux notices" had been posted in the neighborhood of Thebes warning certain people to leave. One of the notes, directed to Azariah L. Smith, read, "Notice is hereby given that any person or persons meddling in any way with any of the Thomas Pettit heirs of the estate, will be hanged. No respecter of persons. By order of the K. K. K. Com."[6] Smith had recently returned to the area and married his ex-wife, who was the widow of Thomas Pettit. A dispute between Smith and his stepson over ownership of a colt led to charges of horse stealing against Smith, and he was arrested. On the night of May 2, 1874, while Smith was in court in Thebes before Justice of the Peace George W. Sammons, a mob of about 40 men entered the room intent on lynching him.[7] They blew out the lights and in the fight that ensued broke the arm of the justice of the peace, but Smith was able to escape and fled to Cairo, the county seat, to turn himself in to the sheriff and gain protection.

Only the names of three men in the "mob" are recorded: Oliver G. Ford, a stepson-in-law of Smith; John Andrew Dolman; and Dazy Breese, who was under indictment and awaiting trial for the murder of his brother in 1873.[8] Although the group called themselves the "K. K. K." and were called "Ku Klux" by the county press, the organization, like similar ones in southern

Illinois, seems to have been more of a vigilante committee, with little in common with the genuine Klan of the South or its political agenda and seems to have sprung into existence from a family feud.

The term Ku Klux Klan had thus taken on a different meaning in southern Illinois by 1874 and was applied to any night-riding vigilante group, not just those whose goal was to "redeem" the South by limiting African American voting and silence demands for equality. The southern Klan and rampant violence against freedmen was a myth, the Cairo newspaper declared in 1868, but in 1874, when violence was perpetrated toward Whites, even the editor of the *Cairo Daily Bulletin* was opposed to it and stated, "The good people of Thebes ought to crush out lawlessness of this kind."[9] Ku Klux Klan activity in southern Illinois, from a real or imagined Klan, was being reported in city newspapers with a national circulation, which not only presented the region as lawless but could hamper its economic growth, political influence, and social progress; for this reason the Klan was opposed by the White press.

What was called the Klan was not limited to Alexander and Pulaski Counties but sprang up in other counties, where it was more active and notorious. During the summer of 1874, a group of about 15 men from the area of Carrier Mills in Saline County began calling themselves Regulators and visiting certain men at night while dressed in robes and hoods to threaten them.[10] They were known as Regulators because they attempted to regulate from outside of the law the private lives of those in their neighborhood. Relationships between wife and husband were subject to regulation, and how children were being raised was subject to oversight and instruction, as well as how well a farmer maintained his crops or paid his bills. The Regulators in southern Illinois, locally called the Ku Klux Klan, were the righteous judges self-appointed to regulate the lives of those in their community.

Late in 1874 disguised men alleged to be the Klan went at night to the home of a White resident of Saline County, took him from his bed, and fired pistols near his feet to make him dance on his porch.[11] The same night, they visited another home in that county and beat the man and threatened to kill him if they had cause to return. A dozen masked so-called Klansmen also visited the house of William Sloan in Johnson County and deposited a bundle of hickory withes at his back door and threatened to return and whip him if rumors of him abusing his children proved true. They returned on January 15, 1875, and gave him a severe flogging of 50 lashes on his back and on the same night visited the home of William Camden in Williamson County.[12] They called Camden out and made him play his fiddle while a young man was made to dance barefoot for about one hour. Also in January 1875, Elias McDaniel, a White man who lived three miles from New Burnside in Johnson County, was visited by what the press called the Klan, who took him from his home and gave him one hundred lashes.

The most notorious "Ku Klux Klan" activity in southern Illinois during the nineteenth century was in Williamson and Franklin Counties and was centered at a community called Sneak Out in Cave Township, about seven and a half miles southeast of Benton in the southeastern corner of Franklin County.[13] They called themselves the Ku Klux Company, the Golden Ring Klan, or The Regulators, and their uniform was "a long white coat trimmed with black, a white cape, also a white cap with a cape reaching below the shoulders—all trimmed with black."[14] Their horses and mules were also covered with white sheets, and a Chicago newspaper account added that the horses wore red and black tassels and the men's white sheets were streaked with red about the eyes and mouth.[15] This southern Illinois version of the Klan had the most similarities to the First Ku Klux Klan of the South. They used the same secret signs, grips, and handshakes that were used by the Ku Klux Klan in Alabama and Mississippi.[16]

The Sneak Out Klan was accused of many incidents of night riding, beatings, and murders. Their most notorious crime was the lynching of Isaac "Lying Ike" Vancil, an elderly White farmer in his 70s, living on Big Muddy River in Williamson County in 1872. Eight men were charged with his murder in Williamson County, but the trial revealed how difficult it was to prosecute Klan members. (Those charged were William Sansom, Francis Marion Gray, Pleasant G. Veach, and Samuel Gossette, all of Herrin's Prairie in Williamson County; and Samuel Sweet, Jonas G. Elliott, John H. Rich, and Jesse H. Cavins, all of Six Mile Prairie in Franklin County.[17]) All the men were acquitted of the murder, mainly because no positive identification could be made, the men all having been disguised.[18] In other cases against the Klan, witnesses were sometimes too intimidated to come forward or left the county so they would not have to testify. The Klan was emboldened and accelerated their night-riding escapades after the murder of Vancil, and two more murders attributed to the Klan occurred after the trial. Two witnesses in the Vancil case, James "Old Jim" Henderson, while plowing in his field, and Milton Colp, were assassinated before the trial.[19]

A decision was made to prosecute the "Ku Klux cases" from Williamson County in federal court under the Ku Klux Klan Act of 1871.[20] Although the intent of the law was to protect the civil rights, especially voting rights, of freedmen, some prosecutors believed the activities of the southern Illinois version of the Klan qualified for prosecution under federal law because they were carried out by a secret vigilante organization that rode around masked under cover of night while on their errands of violence.[21] More than one federal grand jury in Springfield indicted several Klansmen from southern Illinois, but the federal law was never successfully used to convict any Klansmen there. The federal indictments alone were enough to quiet the violence of the Klan for a while.

What finally brought the Sneak Out Klan under control was an armed state militia. Franklin County Sheriff James Frank Mason organized an independent military company at Benton armed with Enfield rifles sent by Illinois Governor John Lourie Beveridge in August 1875 to protect Franklin County citizens against the Klan.[22] Sheriff Noah E. Norris of Williamson County encouraged by the successful work in Franklin County, requested guns, ammunition, and one hundred horses so he could raise a company to fight the Klan in his county.[23] A battle between 14 masked and robed Klansmen and 20 militiamen occurred at the home of Franklin County Commissioner Maddox in which 13 of the Klansmen were wounded.[24] (According to an informant, the Klan members participating that night were Aaron Neal, the leader; Calvin Moore, the oath giver; and George Proctor, George Herd, Wilson Summers, Thomas Sommers Jr., Mardonia Sommers, Henderson Sommers, Rufus Stripling, Williamson W. Briley, William Plasters Jr., Green M. Cantrell, John Wilson Duckworth, and William W. Jacobs.)[25] One of the wounded, thinking he was dying, became an informant, and one by one Klan members were all arrested in the days that followed. The reign of the would-be Klan in southern Illinois was ending.

Forty arrest warrants were issued in Springfield for members of the Sneak Out Klan, and again the decision was to try them in federal court under Ku Klux Klan laws. (Men arrested included Akin Plasters Sr., Enoch Summers, Jasper Newton Neal, Eli Summers, Calvin Summers, Joseph Huffpine, Hiram Summers, William Boyd Jr., Thomas Poage, William Scarlet, Elisha Summers, John Launius, William Launius, Huston Summers, Randall Poindexter, Elias Summers, Calvin Summers, Daniel Summers, Ambrose Summers, Mandex Summers, Marve Shaw, Benjamin Herd, Steven Herd,

William C. Perriman, William Perriman Sr., James Abshear, Lafayette Abshear, William Knight Sr., William Knight Jr., John Vincon, James Bailey, John R. Moore, James Shain, Robert Summers Sr., Scote Summers, Henry Johnson, William Boyd, Henry Johnson, Francis Marion "Frank" Fleming, William Nolen, Aaron Neal, Green M. Cantrell, James Launius, and Williamson Briley.)[26] Federal courts faced roadblocks and the same unwillingness of witnesses to testify because of fear of reprisals. Samuel Treat, United States judge for the southern district of Illinois in Springfield, stated that the federal law did not apply to the Ku Klux Klan cases in southern Illinois because he believed the law only applied to attempts made to deprive citizens of their Fourteenth Amendment and Fifteenth Amendment rights and could only be used in the South in states under military rule.[27] The federal prosecution of the Klan by District Attorney Van Dorston was dropped after his resignation in February 1876. The best that Franklin County State's Attorney William W. Barr could do locally was get a conviction in January 1876 against one man for disturbing the peace on the night of the Klan raid at Maddox Lane.[28]

Jackson County, bordering Williamson and Franklin Counties, also had its own violence from a band of night riders. In full regalia of black robes and hoods, a group of 20 alleged Ku Klux Klan members in Jackson County visited one resident who recognized one man as Montgomery Stevens of Ora Township. Stevens was later captured by Sheriff John B. Kimball and not only confessed to robbery but implicated Jeremiah L. "Jerry" Callahan as the leader.[29] Callahan, a native of County Cork, Ireland, had served in Company B, 21st Alabama Infantry of the Confederate Army, and was discharged for disability in 1864. Although Callahan was a veteran of the Confederate Army, there seems to be no legitimate connection between his group and the southern Ku Klux Klan. This Jackson County organization, although called the Callahan Klan, seems to have only used the robes and hoods of the Knights of the Ku Klux Klan, in this case black instead of white, to disguise their identity while engaged in banditry and highway robbery. They had no other similarities to the First Ku Klux Klan.[30]

State Representative Fountaine E. Albright, of Murphysboro, wrote to Governor Beveridge on August 7, 1875, asking for assistance in fighting what he called the Klan. Albright wrote, "The lawlessness of Bloody Williamson is beginning to slop over into Jackson."[31] A militia company was also organized in Jackson County to fight their disguised "Klan" bandits, although Democratic

Sheriff John B. Kimball did not think it was necessary.[32] The governor shipped one hundred breech-loaders and five thousand cartridges to Jackson County in August 1875, and the armed militia began rounding up known Klan members, just as had been done in Franklin and Williamson Counties. Jeremiah Callahan was arrested, put on trial, and sentenced to 14 years in the state penitentiary for his Klan activity but died on November 30, 1875. An armed militia, necessary or not, put an end to the so-called Ku Klux Klan in Jackson County, just as it had elsewhere in southern Illinois.

The final appearance in southern Illinois during the nineteenth century of any group even weakly resembling the First Ku Klux Klan was in 1879 from a Hardin County group that did not actually call themselves the Ku Klux Klan. In fact, the organization gave itself no name so that its "members could truthfully swear that they 'knew of no Ku-Klux organization in the county.'"[33] If they did not call themselves the Klan, they probably assumed that they could not be prosecuted under the Ku Klux Klan Act as had been done in Franklin and Williamson Counties. As with similar organizations in southern Illinois, they were midnight regulators with secret signs, uniforms, and passwords. "Their faces were to be cowled, and a light was to be carried in the hat of each during a raid on evildoers," the *Louisville Courier Journal* reported in 1879. According to testimony of two witnesses, both former members, the organization was created mainly to assassinate and intimidate witnesses against the infamous outlaw Logan Belt in his trial for murder in Gallatin County. Most members of this group were close relatives to Belt.

Fifteen men were indicted in Hardin County for "unlawful conspiracy (i.e., ku-kluxing)" in May 1879 but were acquitted. Those charged were Logan Belt, Jonathon Belt, Hiram J. Belt, James Belt, Arthur Belt, Elisha Morris, William Fraley, George Ratliffe, Frank Justice (reportedly second captain), Tom Leeper, Robert Sheridan (reportedly first captain), W. D. White, Bill Lyons, Earl Sherwood, and H. Holloman. The two members who testified against the others were Frank Hardin and Benjamin Z. Jenkins.[34] While in jail awaiting trial for the murder of Dock Oldham at a dance in Hardin County, Belt wrote that there had been "a great amount of slush hashed up about the Belts being organized into a Ku-Klux-Klan, all of which is infamously false and has no foundation in truth."[35] Belt was tried for the murder and found guilty of manslaughter at Shawneetown in Gallatin County in July 1879 and was sent to the state penitentiary at Joliet for 15 years.[36] The *Shawneetown Herald* stated, "It is a warning to the revolver-carrying people of Hardin, no matter to what gang they belong, that though 'the mills of the Gods grind slow, they grind exceeding fine.'"[37]

The organizations in southern Illinois during the 1870s that were sometimes called the Ku Klux Klan only had a slight resemblance to the First Ku Klux Klan in the South in that they were secret societies of terrorists and hooded night riders. In fact, most did not even use the name Ku Klux Klan for themselves but were named the Klan by regional newspapers and then national ones as their violence became more notorious and widely known. The goals of the so-called Klan in southern Illinois and that of the South were in stark contrast, and there were almost no examples of terrorism against African Americans in southern Illinois by these groups, at least the few that were reported in the local or national press. In southern Illinois the Klan in the 1870s was most active in counties where there were few African American residents and where Blacks were not seen as a great social or political threat to White supremacy. John Duckworth, a member of the Sneak Out Klan, testified in 1875 that the object of their Klan was "to make fellows do as we wanted them to."[38] W. W. Jacobs, another Klansman from Franklin County, claimed the goal of the Klan was "to do simply as it pleased without regard to law or anything else."[39] Simply put, they were bullies. The *Cairo Bulletin* stated that "the Klan had no political objects in view. Its members were more interested in mischief and bad whiskey and bad women than in affairs of State." In fact, the 50 Klansmen indicted from Franklin County had no common political ideology; they were equally divided between Republicans and Democrats.[40]

Significantly, the southern Illinois Klansmen of the 1870s had no political or social agenda. Although they were similar to the southern Klan in appearance, their acts of violence were almost never centered on outrages against Americans of African descent but were generally perpetrated against White families. They rarely had a racist motivation, but there were a few exceptions. What the editor of the Cairo newspaper called a "Ku-Klux" demonstration occurred in Anna in Union County in October 1874, when some citizens who employed Black workers were notified that "they must discharge all the negroes in their employ and send the negroes out of the county or suffer the consequences."[41] Several miles to the north, in Randolph County, a Black man was taken out of his house during the night, tied to a tree, and whipped on his bare back because he refused to leave the county.[42] J. C. Clark, "teacher of a negro school at Marion," wrote a letter to the *Marion Monitor* in 1874 claiming, "Since I have been teaching, I have had many attacks from my enemies, who swear that no man shall live in this neighborhood and teach the negroes. Some have told me I would not live to get one month taught. I feel that I am in danger of my life."[43]

The naming of the southern Illinois groups of regulators the Ku Klux Klan as early as 1868 was done to draw contrast between terrorism against Americans of African descent in the South and against Americans of European descent in southern Illinois. Some Democratic newspapers tried to discredit Republican rule in the state and the nation by suggesting that the federal and state governments were only interested in prosecuting violence directed toward Black citizens, who usually voted Republican, and ignored that against Whites. When the crimes of the Klan, especially in Williamson County, accumulated and became public, Oberly, the editor of a Democratic Cairo newspaper, ranted, "A dead N——— is the hope of Williamson County. . . . As soon as his stark body is found, the devil will be to pay all over the country, and somebody will be arrested on suspicion even if all the arms of the United States is necessary to make arrest. Dead white men don't have the effect on Radical governors and other office holders; it takes dead N———s to arouse them into law-enforcing action."[44]

Oberly's racially tinted criticism seems unfair. Radical Republicans' national policy focused on protecting Americans of African descent in the South did not equate to not caring about White citizens in southern Illinois. The intent of the Ku Klux Klan Act was to protect the civil rights of freedmen under the Fourteenth and Fifteenth Amendments in former Confederate states that had begun rejoining the Union in 1868. Under federalism, state governments were expected to take the lead in protecting their citizens, White and Black, rather than the national government, but when states were lax in prosecutions, the federal government could step in. Oberly's criticism should have been directed more locally to inefficient sheriffs and state's attorneys and juries who refused to indict and convict. It was a Republican governor, John L. Beveridge, who armed local militias in southern Illinois counties in 1875 that brought an end to Klan-like vigilante groups' rule there.

The press and some prosecutors later believed that by labeling the southern Illinois groups of night riders the Ku Klux Klan they could more easily prosecute them under the federal Klan laws. This is most clearly evident in the prosecution of the Sneak Out Klan in Franklin County. Federal prosecution proved just as fruitless, but it was the last resort at trying to bring southern Illinois Klan members to justice under the law.

The press of southern Illinois in the 1870s generally ridiculed the so-called Klan in the region and spoke out for law and order and an end to the vigilantism attributed to them. Klansmen were outlaws, murderers, bandits, and highway robbers, and as late as the 1920s there were many White citizens who had personal memories about the so-called Klan in southern Illinois who could testify to their atrocities. Thousands of Black citizens in the South and some who had moved to southern Illinois could testify to the horrors and outrages committed against them by the First Ku Klux Klan, one might argue the legitimate Klan. Now, a little more than 25 years after the last night ride was made in southern Illinois by any group called by itself or the press the Ku Klux Klan, a different version of history was being presented. Thomas Dixon's books and plays and similar ones by other authors represented the Klan as the heroes of White America and the protectors of White womanhood, and many were willingly duped into believing the myth or at least pretending that they did. The time was becoming ripe for organizing the Second Ku Klux Klan in the nation and in southern Illinois.

CHAPTER THREE

The Second Coming of the Klan

THE GROUNDWORK WAS DONE and the stage was set for the coming of what historians refer to as the Second Ku Klux Klan. David Wark (D. W.) Griffith adapted Thomas Dixon's novel and play, *The Clansman*, to produce his influential film *The Birth of a Nation*, which was released in theaters across America in 1915. The movie followed the theme of the novel and glorified the First Ku Klux Klan of the 1870s and the monstrous acts committed against African Americans. The film portrayed the Klan as the savior of the White South and in particular White womanhood from Black rule and domination. In one scene, Flora Cameron, a young White woman, jumps to her death to avoid her pursuer, Gus, a former slave who had become a federal army officer. At the climax of the motion picture, the Klansmen on horseback chase down and lynch Gus, played in blackface by a White actor, often to the yells and cheers of many in the audience. Only months after the film was released, it became the inspiration for what historians call the Second Ku Klux Klan. The timing was right for the rebirth of the KKK.

The Knights of the Ku Klux Klan was revived on Thanksgiving Day, 1915, atop Stone Mountain outside of Atlanta, Georgia, by a small group of men led by the Reverend William Joseph Simmons, a former Methodist Episcopal minister. They built an altar, on which they laid an American flag, a Bible, and a sword; set fire to a cross; and recreated the "Invisible Empire." From its beginning, the Second Ku Klux Klan used Protestant Christianity and Christian symbols to spread its message of salvation of America through hatred of everything they called un-American. The Second Klan was here to rescue America, they claimed, just like the First Klan had redeemed the South from Black rule before its gradual disappearance in the late nineteenth century.

Simmons, who had been suspended from the ministry by the Methodist Episcopal Church for "inefficiency" and who at times struggled with his excessive use of alcohol, wrote in 1916 that "only good Christian white people" preaching racial purity and Protestant morality could save America from coming destruction. Simmons worked for such fraternal organizations as Woodmen of the World, Masonic Lodge, Knights of Pythias, and Independent Order of Odd Fellows, but he dreamed of founding a fraternal order based on White male bonding through racism.[1] The message the Klan would preach was White supremacy, Protestant Christianity, and extreme Christian nationalism. The official creed of the Knights of the Ku Klux Klan perpetuated the myth of race and stated, "We avow the distinction between the races of mankind as same has been decreed by the Creator, and we shall ever be true in the faithful maintenance of White Supremacy and will strenuously oppose any compromise thereof in any and all things."[2]

By 1920 Simmons had convinced several hundred men to join the Klan, but it was his decision that year to hire Elizabeth Tyler and Edward Young Clark as publicity agents, which skyrocketed Klan membership and established a system of payment of dues and fees to the Klan hierarchy. Tyler and Clark were promised 80 percent of the revenue they generated by new membership.[3] They convinced Simmons to expand the Klan's bigotry beyond that directed at Americans of African descent and begin a massive media advertising campaign. Under their guidance the Klan grew from a few hundred members to 850,000 by the summer of 1921.[4]

In their desire to expand the Klan and thereby increase their own wealth, Tyler and Clark saw the Ku Klux Klan as a business that was growing but not meeting its potential, and Simmons as a drunkard and a hindrance to membership expansion. In a coup they took over the Klan organization and put in Hiram Evans of Texas to replace Simmons as the new imperial wizard in November 1922. Simmons was officially banished in January 1924 from the Klan that he had created, which led to a legal battle between the new leader Evans and Simmons over control of Klan property.[5]

To gain members, the country was divided into nine territories, each headed by a grand dragon. Salaried solicitors called "kleagles" were sent into the areas to recruit members. Recruiters usually started with local Masonic Lodge membership lists and from there contacted Protestant church pastors, especially among the Methodist, Baptist, and Christian (Disciples of Christ) denominations. Ministers were offered free membership, and some became "kludds," or chaplains, of local klaverns.

The entrance fee for nonclergymen to join was ten dollars, called a "klec-token," four dollars of which was kept by the solicitor as a commission for his work.[6] Members then had to pay five dollars in annual dues and purchase the Klan hood and robe costume for $6.50, which was only available through the national organization. The Klan mostly attracted middle-class Protestant men, business owners, and well-to-do farmers, and also better educated ministers, teachers, lawyers, and doctors. Membership became a status symbol. There were also millions of poor White men who agreed with the goals of the Klan and supported it from the sidelines but did not have the $21.50 (the equivalent of about $375 in 2023) to pay the initiation fee, annual dues, and cost of the costume.

The Klan getup had to be official, and no homemade robes were allowed. The costume consisted of a full-length robe with the official insignia of the cross within a circle over the right breast, a sash to tie around the waist, a cone-shaped helmet or hood with a red tassel hanging from the top, a piece of cloth with eye holes cut out to hang across the front of the hood, and another piece of cloth to hang from the hood to the shoulders in the back. It was an exciting and proud day for the local Klan when the robes and hoods were distributed to members.

The message that appealed to those who joined was not only White supremacy but that America needed a revival of its traditional, conservative moralism, or "old-time religion," to confront the perceived rise in crime and immorality. In their eyes, the America that White Protestants had controlled and dominated from the beginning was unraveling and falling apart. It was a time when many White Protestants opposed the teaching of evolution in public schools because it threatened their faith and ideals and when fear culminated in the famous Scopes Trial in Tennessee in 1925. There was a near paranoia level of fear over rising numbers of "new immigrants" from southern and eastern Europe, who were more likely to be Roman Catholic, Eastern Orthodox, or Jewish than Protestant Christian. The growth of organized labor and labor unions scared them. Bootleggers, who were violating Prohibition laws, and local gangsters, like the Charlie Birger Gang and the Shelton Brothers, were running rampant, while sheriffs in some southern Illinois counties looked the other way and seemed to be in league with the criminals.

The spread of communism and socialism led to the "Red Scare" of 1919–20. Although Eugene Debs, the leader of the Socialist Party, made a visit to Cairo and spoke at the opera house in 1906, the Socialist Party had peaked in the teens, and by the 1920s the party had no candidates for county offices on the ballots in Alexander or Pulaski County.[7]

The Second Klan thus promoted White nationalism, White supremacy, and a return to traditional values in a way that did not openly call for race hatred or support violence against Americans of African descent. William J. Simmons, in testifying before the House Rules Committee in 1921 while he was still at the head of the Klan, falsely stated the Ku Klux Klan had "never taken the law into its own hands."[8] Despite the reassurance of Simmons, when the Ku Klux Klan spread hateful rhetoric against Americans of African descent and immigrants, violence followed.

The fears and concerns promoted by the Ku Klux Klan were not universal, but potential Klan members could pick through the bag of Klan causes and find something in the rhetoric to support and ignore the rest. Klaverns focused on whatever enemy worked best for them locally to acquire membership—although the Ku Klux Klan could never be separated from racism and its rhetoric of White supremacy.

Klan membership was promoted as small-town, wholesome family fun. They had picnics, and the secrecy and mystical names and titles of the Knights of the Klan made membership initially new and exciting for its members. It provided Klansmen camaraderie with other like-minded community members and neighbors and gave members a sense of belonging. It also provided money for local Protestant churches and became a way for making business connections and gaining political support. In Illinois, the impetus started in larger cities. The Klan organized local klaverns first in Chicago, Springfield, and East St. Louis, and then through much of rural and small-town southern Illinois. One of the keys to the success of the Ku Klux Klan was its regional adaptability.

The first mention of an initiation meeting in Chicago was on August 16, 1921, when ten thousand allegedly met, but the efforts to organize had been going on for months before.[9] Some state officials saw the dangers of the Ku Klux Klan as the organization steadily expanded in urban areas of Illinois, almost exclusively in the northern part of the state. The Illinois General Assembly passed a resolution in June 1921 condemning the efforts of the Ku Klux

Klan to organize in Illinois.[10] The resolution was introduced by Hon. Shead-rick B. Turner, a Chicago representative of African descent.[11] The resolution stated,

> Whereas, it is reported that there are representatives of the Ku Klux Klan attempting to organize chapters or posts of that organization in various cities of the state of Illinois and Whereas it is believed that the Ku Klux Klan is an organization which operates in defiance of law and order and against the best interests and welfare of the people at large; now, therefore, be it Resolved by the house of representatives of the state of Illinois, that we condemn and deplore the attempt to organize posts of the Ku Klux Klan in the state of Illinois and urge all good citizens of the state in the interest of law and order and the welfare of our state to do everything in their power to force its foremost leaders to refrain from attempting to stir up racial strife within the confines of Illinois.[12]

In May 1923 the Abraham Lincoln Klavern of the Ku Klux Klan held an initiation ceremony at the coliseum at the state fairgrounds in Springfield, and the celebration lasted until 4 A.M.[13] The Klan's recruitment efforts were gaining attention, and public opposition to the Klan also continued to grow. Governor Len Small signed a bill in June 1923 that prohibited public masking—that is, wearing the white, pointed hoods of the Klan that con-cealed their identities—but it was not often enforced. Small, of Kankakee, the most corrupt governor in Illinois history, was acquitted in 1925 on embezzle-ment charges, and 8 of the 12 jurors who exonerated him were rewarded with state jobs. But despite his initial opposition to the Klan, Small was soon won over, and the Klan endorsed his reelection campaigns in 1924, 1928, and 1932, although with each election the Klan's influence over voters weakened as its membership diminished.[14]

National membership had risen to over one million by 1922, and within three years the Ku Klux Klan claimed to have close to five million dues-paying members. The statistics are questionable, and most historians believe that the Klan exaggerated its numbers in press releases to make people want to be a part of a rising new movement, join the bandwagon, and not be left out. Even if the numbers were exaggerated, the national appeal of the Klan was obvious: the heart of the popularity of the Second Klan was the Mid-west and not the Old South, and it had more members from urban areas than rural ones. Eventually membership rose to the level to which, in

June 1923, Illinois became a self-governing realm of the Ku Klux Klan.[15] Charles Grover Palmer, an attorney in Chicago, was made its grand dragon. By 1924, 40 percent of total membership in the Invisible Empire of the Knights of the Ku Klux Klan could be found in Indiana, Ohio, and Illinois.[16]

Some of the enthusiasm to sign up with the Klan was driven by the fact that 1924 was a presidential election year. The Indiana Klan officially endorsed Republican candidate Calvin Coolidge, but the national organization did not openly support him as it did not want to offend southern Democrats. Meanwhile, the Democrats' presidential candidate, John W. Davis, condemned the Klan in order to maintain support from Catholics and immigrants.[17] There was also interest in a Klan-supported bill which, when signed into law by President Coolidge on May 26, 1924, severely limited the number of immigrants from southern and eastern Europe.

A Klan organizer was assigned to Jackson, Williamson, and Franklin counties in Illinois and began work in Murphysboro in August 1922.[18] Recruitment began in Williamson County at least by November 1922, and membership drives were stepped up the following year. On February 24, 1923, robed Klan members entered the Presbyterian church in Centralia in Marion County and the Methodist church in Murphysboro in Jackson County while services were in session.[19] On May 20, 1923, 17 robed Klansmen walked quietly and orderly in a single file into First Christian Church of Marion in Williamson County and handed three ten-dollar bills to Charles Reign Scoville, a nationally acclaimed evangelist for the Church of Christ Disciples. By the time robed Klansmen made a public appearance in church, they had already been in the community for weeks secretly recruiting among fraternal organizations and Protestant church leaders. The scene was no doubt choreographed for effect, and only five days later around midnight at a meeting of about two thousand people, two hundred men were initiated into the mysteries of the Invisible Empire outside of Marion.

The letter that was addressed and presented to the Reverend Scoville at the revival meeting gives insight into the immediate goals of the Klan in that part of southern Illinois.

Dear Sir:
Please accept this token of our appreciation of your efforts and great work you are doing for this community. The Knights of the Ku Klux

Klan are behind this kind of work to a man and stand for the highest
ideals of the native born white Gentile American citizenship which are:

The tenets of the Christian religion; protection of pure womanhood;
just laws and liberty; absolute upholding of the Constitution of the
United States; free public schools; free speech; free press and law and
order.

Yours for a better and greater community,
Exalted Cyclops[20]

In August 1923, about one hundred new members were initiated into the
Klan at DuQuoin in Perry County. Cars with the "fiery cross" emblem on
their radiators led a procession through the town. Each car with the emblem
led the parade of delegates from their klavern, with about five hundred participating. They met in a field and burned a cross at the beginning of the ceremony. The editor of the *Jonesboro Gazette* in Union County stated, "There
is little doubt that the Klan is being established and that its membership in
all southern Illinois counties is growing rapidly. Counties all around Du-
Quoin are reported to have a large membership and it is said that the
organizers claim that a million Illinois men will be enlisted by the end of
the year."[21]

Just a week later, there was a gigantic "open-air meeting" of between five
and ten thousand Klansmen representing 35 southern Illinois towns on the
outskirts of West Frankfort on the "hard road" toward Benton.[22] A 69-foot
cross was lighted about midnight that could be seen for miles, and the automobiles encircled the cross and turned on their headlights, which made it as
bright as day. Over 250 men were sworn in as new members. The *Herrin Journal* stated, "The Knights of the Ku Klux Klan are becoming very strong in
Southern Illinois."

Each local Klan organization took on its own character, and in Williamson County the work of the Klan focused on enforcing Prohibition.[23] They
hired Seth Glenn Young to come to Williamson County and work separately
from the sheriff and other law enforcement officers to raid bootleggers and
joints illegally selling alcohol. Young worked with support of Klan members
throughout southwestern Illinois, rounding up bootleggers and raiding stills,
and the *Cairo Evening Citizen* stated that Young was "remembered in Cairo
as the most fearless and daring Prohibition enforcement officer that ever
worked here."[24]

The rhetoric from the Williamson County Klan was also anti-Catholic and opposed organized labor, especially in the coal mines, where many miners were immigrants. In fact, the Klan was xenophobic and went so far as to call for the expulsion from the United States of "non-Nordic races" meaning all but Anglo-Saxons and Germanic people from northern Europe with light eyes, hair, and skin.[25] In 1923, when Father Ermenegildo Senese, a native of Italy who immigrated in 1904, was leading efforts to build a new Catholic church in Herrin, Our Lady of Mt. Carmel Church, the Reverend Philip Rutherford Glotfelty Sr. of the Methodist Episcopal church in Herrin in a sermon accused the members of Father Senese's church, a majority of them Italian immigrants, of being mostly bootleggers.[26]

Klan activity was most notorious in Williamson County, which again became known as "Bloody Williamson," a name given to the county during violent "Klan" activities in the 1870s. There the efforts of the Klan focused on the enforcement of Prohibition by stamping out bootleggers and roadhouses in the county, and there Young gained a reputation as a heroic crime fighter for the local Klan.[27] When Governor Small was running for reelection in 1924, Young was invited to campaign with him in southern Illinois.[28]

Thus, the growth of the Illinois Ku Klux Klan started in Chicago and moved south, reaching southern Illinois by the fall of 1922. Once the work of the Klan missionaries proved successful in Williamson, Franklin, Perry, and Jackson counties, it was only a matter a time before the Klan moved into Pulaski and Alexander counties, where it found more fertile ground for recruitment. There the focus would not be xenophobia or religious bigotry but the widely accepted standby of old-time Protestantism and racist White supremacy.

CHAPTER FOUR

Pulaski and Alexander Counties in 1923

WHEN THE KU KLUX KLAN began recruitment in Pulaski and Alexander counties in 1923, they moved into a region that was rural and dominated by agriculture. Sixty-three percent of the population of Pulaski County in 1920 lived on farms, while 37 percent of those in Alexander County were farmers or farm laborers.[1] Corn and wheat were the dominant crops, but a few farmers had begun experimenting with cotton in the mid-1920s, and Villa Ridge was known for vegetable and fruit production, especially strawberries, which had been shipped to northern markets by rail since the 1860s. Retail businesses prospered in both counties, and neither was without industry, meager though it was. But at the center of the economy was agriculture, and when farmers suffered financially, their situation trickled down to other businesses.

Cairo, the county seat of Alexander, was the one factor that made that county different from its neighbor. The small city was less tied to agriculture and more prosperous than the rest of the region, but Prohibition had given it a hard punch, causing all the saloons, bars, and brewing companies to go out of business or be converted into speakeasies or legal business ventures. Professional gamblers who drifted in and out of town found alternative establishments outside city limits to carry on their activities, and the usual complaints were voiced against the houses of prostitution along Thirteenth Street, which had gained a national reputation since the Civil War. The beer brewery was gone, but the town had four bottling companies in 1923, three for soft drinks and one for milk products. Retail businesses attracted many visitors to town and was now the heart of the community's prosperity. The town had nearly 100 small retail grocery stores, 13 drug stores, 13 confectioneries, 10 clothing stores, 6 shoe shops, and 6 bakeries, as well as 30 restaurants, 24 barbershops, 13 hotels, 7 pool halls, 6 taxi companies, and 6 cigar and tobacco shops.[2] The rest of the county outside of Cairo was agrarian and re-markably similar to Pulaski County.

Second in importance to agriculture in the region was the lumber indus-try, which although beginning to decline by 1923, still employed several hun-dred workers in saw mills and lumber camps in both counties. Some of the timber the mills used was beginning to be brought upriver from the South as the local forest resources became depleted.[3] Cairo had several factories con-nected to the lumber industry, including a Singer sewing machine company, which made cabinets for the machines, and a Singer veneer manufacturing company. The Illinois Lumber Company, known as the Sears Roebuck Mill, north of Cairo and outside the protection of the levee, produced lumber for Sears ready-cut home kits. Also connected to the lumber industry were the Ullin Box Company owned by Lewis H. Needham and Main Brothers Box and Lumber Company in Karnak, which produced wooden crates used mostly in shipping agriculture products. There was also a stave mill, veneer mill, and furniture company along the riverfront in Mound City, which had about half the number of jobs in the lumber industry as Cairo, although Mound City had only about one-fifth of the population of its neighbor.

Mound City also had a hoop mill that produced metal hoops used in bar-rel making and a canning factory that combined employed about one hun-dred people with seasonable jobs. Cairo was more closely tied to the river industry, having immediate access to the Mississippi and Ohio Rivers, but the Marine Ways were located at Mound City. Created in 1859 with its dry docks, the shipyard was still operating and employed dozens of men who took steam-ers and diesel boats out of the water for repairs. In 1929, the completion of the Olmsted lock and dam, which began construction in 1926, would further connect the economy of Pulaski County to the Ohio River.

Railroads in both counties remained very influential and, next to agricul-ture and the lumber industry, employed the most workers. Trains were the most common mode of transportation in the state at that time, and locally a seven-mile interurban train line ran a daily and nightly schedule that con-nected Cairo and Mound City and then extended four miles farther north into Mounds. There were large railroad yards in Cairo, Mounds, and Tamms, where many men found employment. The trains still stopped at depots in each town along their routes to load and unload shipments and pick up and drop off passengers. Since the Supreme Court ruling in *Plessy v. Ferguson* in 1896, segregation had spread across the land. Passenger cars in Illinois were still integrated, but Black citizens in Alexander and Pulaski counties traveling south or west out of the state were ushered out of cars marked "This car for white passengers only" and to rear coaches marked "colored only."[4] After northbound trains crossed the river into Illinois, the signs were supposed to be taken down for passenger cars continuing north.

The silica mines and mills in Elco and Tamms employed close to 50 people in 1920 and remained stable employers through the decade. Another major industry outside of Cairo was the dynamite plant at Fayville, which employed 90 workers in 1920.[5] These jobs were the highest paid in the county for laborers, but they were extremely dangerous. A large explosion at the plant, which killed several workers and damaged many of the buildings in 1923, was an economic blow to the county. The business never recovered, the Fayville Post Office was closed in 1928, and by 1930 the site was a ghost town. Another small but stable employer in Alexander County through the 1920s was the gravel pit near Tamms, which employed about 25 laborers. Between Ullin and Wetaug in Pulaski County there were also two limestone quarry pits, a rock crusher, and a lime kiln that hired Black and White workers by the dozens. But for every laborer in a quarry, sawmill, factory, or retail business in the two counties, there were at least two working on a farm for a dollar a day or less.

The population of Pulaski County in 1923 was about 14,700.[6] Every precinct in Pulaski County had Black residents, and Americans of African descent in the county totaled close to five thousand in 1923, about one-third of the county's population.[7] The largest town was Mound City, the county seat, which had a population of about 2,670, but Mounds was not far behind with about 2,450 residents. Other smaller towns and villages in the county included Ullin, Pulaski, Villa Ridge, Karnak, Grand Chain, Olmsted, Perks, America, and Wetaug, each with several hundred residents.

The population of Alexander County in 1923 was about 23,400.[8] It had a greater population than Pulaski County because of the size of its county seat, Cairo, where 14,500 people, over half the county's population, resided. A majority of Americans of African descent in the county lived in Cairo. Alexander County had several precincts with no African American population, including Delta, East Cape Girardeau, Elco, McClure, and Thebes.[9] There were about 6,500 Americans of African descent living in Alexander County in 1923 comprising about 29 percent of the population in the county.[10] Cairo dominated the county, but there were other smaller incorporated towns in Alexander County, including Thebes and Tamms, and smaller unincorporated villages, namely Olive Branch, Elco, McClure, Unity, Sandusky, Future City, East Cape Girardeau, and Fayville.

The Ohio and Mississippi Rivers brought commerce to Alexander and Pulaski Counties, but they also posed an unpredictable threat of flooding. The 1913 flood was particularly devasting, although Cairo remained protected behind its levee walls. Mound City was also surrounded by an earthen levee protecting it from the Ohio and Cache Rivers, where waters backed up in times of flood, but the town was not as secure as Cairo and did not have a concrete flood wall built on top of the levee. The Pulaski County sheriff, county judge, and mayor of Mound City appealed to Governor Edward Dunne in 1913: "The water of the Ohio River is near the top of the levee. The danger is very imminent and pressing. We appeal for immediate help. Send 10,000 sacks and two companies of militia."[11] The National Guard companies were sent to patrol the town and help sandbag, but it was the five hundred employees sent by the Big Four Railroad who saved the levee and thus Mound City.[12] For both Cairo and Mound City, the rivers were their close economic friends but could also quickly become their greatest enemies, the extent of which they did not realize until the Great Flood of 1937. The threat of flooding was a significant factor that discouraged more industry from moving into the region.

Due to the hard times faced by farmers in the 1920s, a small number resorted to bootlegging to increase their income by running illegal stills in both counties. In the 1920s the price of corn was about a dollar a bushel, and the prices got as low as forty-five cents a bushel in the 1930s, while moonshiners might get fifteen dollars per gallon for corn whiskey.[13] Almost everyone knew a bootlegger and knew where they could purchase illegal alcohol if they wanted it. Prohibition had not ended the consumption of alcohol; it just made the manufacturing, transporting, and selling of it a crime. Bootlegging was dangerous and risky, and during the 14 years of Prohibition (January 1920–December 1933), local newspapers were dotted with stories about arrests of well-known bootleggers, raids of stills, and trials and sentencings in court.

In Alexander County, bootlegging went on with the knowledge and consent of Sheriff Leslie Bronson Roche, who was elected in 1926 following his father, Sheriff James Stephen Roche. Before he became sheriff, Deputy Leslie B. Roche began selling police protection to bootleggers, allegedly without his father's knowledge.[14] Moonshiner George B. Crawford was tried and convicted five times for bootlegging in Alexander County but kept the business going when not serving a jail sentence. He testified in federal court that in 1923 Leslie Roche informed him that he knew about his illegal activities and his associates and said, "I'll be around every month and you can hand me over $100."[15] Crawford complained he had not gotten the protection he had paid for, and since he was arrested five times it seems he was correct. Deputy Richard Fitzgerald stated in court that the protection fee was one dollar a gallon, which was split between him and Roche. Crawford also testified that he had purchased liquor from Leslie Roche for fifteen dollars a gallon, which was delivered to him in five-gallon demijohns, the exchange always happening in secret behind the Iron Mountain Railroad depot in Cairo.

Most of this information was not publicly known until the summer of 1928 when federal Prohibition agent Victor J. Dowd completed his investigation and made arrests. In December of that year, Leslie Roche and 72 other defendants from Alexander County were tried and convicted in federal court in East St. Louis for violating the Volstead Act.[16] One hundred and seven witnesses were called by the government, and it was one of the largest trials in East St. Louis, but in 1923 their criminal activities had just started, and most of the public was unaware of what their sheriff's son was doing.

Before Prohibition became national law, the "drys" led by the Anti-Saloon League and the "wets" fought for dominance in the towns and precincts in Alexander and Pulaski Counties following a 1906 state law that gave voters the "local option" to vote on the issue. In Pulaski County, every precinct voted a ban on the sale of alcohol except Wetaug, but it was always a back-and-forth struggle between the factions at the polls in the region.[17] Prohibition was not popular in the larger towns of Alexander and Pulaski Counties, which could have voted themselves "dry" even before Prohibition had they chosen but generally did not. In the 1907 vote in Cairo, the result was 4,505 in favor of keeping saloons to 653 against.[18] Cairo in particular lost thousands of dollars for each year of Prohibition during which it could not collect fees for liquor licenses.[19] Mound City voted itself dry in 1904 but only by buying votes at two dollars each, and then only to discover that those who wanted to drink rode the few miles outside of town to the Halfway House, a notorious tavern so named because it was halfway between Cairo and Mound City.[20] After the two-year experiment, Mound City voted itself "wet" again and stayed that way until Prohibition.

The Second Ku Klux Klan used the rise in crime ushered in by Prohibition to recruit members in other southern Illinois counties like Williamson, but the tactic was not as successful in Alexander or Pulaski. Many of those who were abstainers used their position against alcohol to justify their membership in the Klan, which they ironically saw as standing for law and order. Klan members who took an occasional drink or consumed even more than that could ignore the Klan rhetoric when it turned to supporting Prohibition.

The message that worked best for Klan recruitment in Pulaski and Alexander Counties was the same one used in the South. People visiting or passing through the counties in 1923 might comment on the southern character of the region and the southern accents of the people, especially in Cairo, "the gateway to the South." Like in the South, the color line was clearly drawn, and in most places in the two counties Jim Crow was alive and well. Segregation was most clearly evident in the areas of religion and education. The 1922 city directory of Cairo, for instance, listed 14 churches labeled "white" and 17 labeled "colored," and that separation was found in every community in both counties. The directory listed seven "white schools" and six "colored schools" in Cairo, which included Sumner High School, one of the earliest high schools opened in the nation for students of African descent and the only high school Black students could attend in Alexander County until Sandusky High School opened in the late 1920s.[21]

An 1872 Illinois law guaranteed African American children access to public education but provided that it could be in separate schools if the local school boards decided. In some cases economic factors won out over the desire to keep the races separate, when taxpayers did not want to fund two separate school systems in the same district. Hoffner School at Pea Ridge near Wetaug was one such rural integrated public school. There in 1893 White students refused to drink from the same water bucket as Black students, so the teacher acquired a "separate but equal" bucket, which Black students then refused to use.[22] How the dilemma was resolved is unclear, but the Wetaug correspondent of the *Cairo Citizen* reported a few weeks after the controversy started that "the pupils of the Hoffner School have buried the hatchet and are all drinking from the same water bucket."[23]

Education for Pulaski County Americans of African descent was usually segregated in the 1920s, and Grand Chain was the only other school district in the county to be integrated. In 1920 there were 24 students of African descent in the village of Grand Chain and 76 attending from the rural precinct. Later, in the 1930s, Black parents insisted that Black students from Grand Chain be sent to the segregated high school in Mound City, where they thought they could get a better education.[24] Both Lovejoy High School in Mound City and Douglass High School in Mounds were segregated schools for students of African descent. The integration of high schools was not a significant issue for the majority of the residents in the region in 1923, as few people, White or Black, were educated beyond the eighth grade.

History from the perspective of people of African descent is typically absent from most public histories of the region, which focused largely on White residents.[25] A notable exception is *Living in Cache Bottom* by Lillian Nesbitt Butler, who was born in 1914 on a farm near the village of Pulaski. Her book provides a firsthand account of life in Pulaski County for African Americans in the 1920s. She wrote, "Racial issues divided the blacks and whites during this period of 'Jim Crow' segregation. To enable one to survive, a tremendous emphasis was placed upon self-improvement through hard work and education. . . . We, Blacks, lived in humble houses in a small town mid a 'Cache Bottom.' . . . Black women worked in the whites' household and farmed fields; it was the only source of money. Receiving small pay, hand-me-down clothes and spoiled smoke meat were gladly received as pay for working for the whites."[26] She remembered that Black families were not allowed to have telephones in their homes, which she thought might have contributed to her father's death, but noted that she learned to view racist Whites not as enemies but racism as a challenge to be overcome.[27]

Thus the Ku Klux Klan found in Alexander and Pulaski Counties a region clearly divided along racial lines. Even in death they were separated, with Cairo City Cemetery in Villa Ridge and cemeteries in Mounds and Ullin being segregated. Nearby Mound City National Cemetery was also segregated during this time and continued so until President Harry S. Truman desegregated the U.S. military in 1948. Elsewhere in the two counties, there were separate cemeteries for Blacks and Whites. Prejudice went hand in hand with segregation and fueled ignorance and fear. This was fertile ground for the Ku Klux Klan to reap the rewards of membership from the seeds of White supremacy and Black submission that had been sowed in the region since its beginnings.

CHAPTER FIVE

The Klan Goes to Church

IN THE SUMMER OF 1923, Klan meetings were first held in Pulaski County, although work at recruitment must have been going on weeks earlier.[1] Meetings were held the second week of September 1923 at Karnak, at Mounds, and at the Grange Hall in Villa Ridge.[2] To gain entrance to the closed meetings, attendees had to pass by guards and know the secret password for that night. Hundreds of cars were noticed at each gathering, and headlights were used to light the meeting and add to the drama of the occasion.

Forrest Hazel Moreland of southern Indiana was appointed the kleagle, or recruiting officer, for the Ku Klux Klan in Pulaski County and probably Alexander County as well and was paid four dollars for each member he recruited.[3] Born out of wedlock in 1895 in Shoals, Indiana, Forrest Hazel Bullock took the name of his stepfather, William S. Moreland, who married Forrest's mother when Forrest was four. By the age of 15 he was a coal miner in Stockton, Indiana. He enlisted in the United States Army in 1916, served through World War I, and was honorably discharged on March 5, 1919. After leaving the army, he spent months as a patient at the U.S. Marine Hospital in Evansville, Indiana. When he came to Pulaski County in 1923, he was single, but in Grand Chain he met and married 23-year-old Rossie Edna Merchant, a teacher in the integrated public school. She came from a prominent family in the area, her father being a well-known local farmer, and her uncle, a lawyer who would be elected Pulaski County state's attorney in 1924.

An open meeting of the Ku Klux Klan, which could be attended by non-members, was held on September 13, 1923, at Grand Chain on Main Street in which about eight hundred attended.[4] Moreland was the main speaker and assured the audience that atrocities and crimes attributed to the Klan in Louisiana and Oklahoma that had been widely reported in local and national newspapers were mere propaganda: "There were no murders in Louisiana. The governor of that state was merely a political tool working to satisfy his aspirations for the presidential nomination." The use of demagoguery, the appealing to emotions and prejudices rather than reason, was a crucial recruiting tool for the Klan.[5] Moreland used allegations of "fake news" and conspiracy theories. He did not tell the audience the truth, and many, no doubt, believed him.

The Louisiana murders to which he referred were not what has come to be called "fake news." One can only speculate whether Moreland believed the falsehoods he was spreading or was deliberately deceiving his audience to gain new members. Two White, outspoken anti-Klan citizens of Mer Rouge, Louisiana, were kidnapped and murdered there in August 1922.[6] The slayings gained national media attention and outrage in a way that the lynching of 51 Americans of African descent the same year had not. Louisiana Governor John M. Parker requested the federal government get involved when local and state officials would not investigate the crime. An inquiry by the Federal Bureau of Investigation led to the arrest of the local Klan leader in 1923, but the parish grand jury refused to indict him. The ordeal, however, brought the Ku Klux Klan into the court of national public opinion, and the Klan was put on the defensive.

Moreland told his audience, "That petty, corrupting, two-by-four Governor Walton of Oklahoma is one of the worst of law violators. That piece of cheese applied for membership in the Klan, but we wouldn't admit him on account of his immorality." He was referring to Democrat James C. "Jack" Walton, governor of Oklahoma elected as a farmer-labor candidate and endorsed by the Socialist Party. He was governor during the Tulsa race riot in 1921. The riot occurred following a violent encounter between a group of armed Black men who had gone to the Tulsa jail to help prevent a lynching of a young Black man falsely accused of rape by a White lynch mob. The rioting that followed lasted 18 hours and left perhaps hundreds dead and thousands homeless. Several months later, Klan recruitment began in earnest in Tulsa and other parts of Oklahoma. To crack down on the Klan, Governor Walton declared martial law, and the National Guard defended some public buildings with machine guns. Walton's political error was in overextending his authority, and when he tried to censor newspapers and suspended *habeas corpus*, both violations of the U.S. and state constitutions, it led to his removal from office in October 1923.[7] At the time of the Grand Chain Klan meeting, a grand jury to investigate Walton had just been formed, and the governor had declared absolute martial law for all of Oklahoma in order to resist the Klan.

Some men in Moreland's audience on September 13 voiced reluctance to join an organization in which they were required to hide behind a mask and asked why the group had to be secretive. Moreland assured them that the reason Klansmen were disguised in masks was not to hide their identity out of shame or to prevent prosecution for illegal activities but to "slip up on the unsuspecting law violator and assist the sheriff and law enforcement officers." Many Klansmen were incredibly open and candid about their membership in the Klan, but it was a secret organization where people who wanted to join secretly could do so.

At the same Grand Chain meeting, the Reverend William Paul Anderson of the First Christian Church in Cairo spoke, comparing the United States with the Roman Empire just before its fall. He seems to have already been a Klan member by the time the Klan visited his church on the evening of October 9, 1923, while he was preaching.[8] His sermon was titled "Is America God's Chosen Nation?" and his text was Hebrews 13:1, "Let brotherly love continue." Anderson believed that God had chosen America to enlighten the world, but the land had become infested with "anti-Americans who are not living in brotherly love, but are grabbing all they can get for themselves." Among the "anti-Americans" were owners of "picture shows" who opened their doors on Sundays. The sermon condemning anti-Americans was the same rhetoric used by the Klan in their propaganda.

Anderson could not have been surprised when robed Klansmen walked down the aisle of his church during service and presented him with a "large sum of money." This tactic had been used elsewhere to recruit church members, but this was the first time it is known to have been done in Pulaski or Alexander County. Millions of dollars were flowing into the Klan's treasury, so investing some of that capital to gain the local clergyman's voice from the pulpit was a sound investment.

Many Protestant ministers joined the Ku Klux Klan and preached the gospel of White supremacy and Black submission, but some had delivered that message even before the Klan arrived. John MacLeod Sutherland was pastor of Pilgrim Congregational Church in Mound City from 1900 to 1904 and also pastored a church in Villa Ridge. His novel, *Then Cometh the Devil*, was published in New York in 1907 and told of his experiences in what he called "the sportiest town on the river" (Mound City).[9] A native of Canada, he wrote about the southern man's prejudices but also confronted his own when he arrived in Mound City:

> Eat food that a negro cooked? Receive his dinner from a negro waiter? He had all the Northern man's prejudice against the darky near at hand. His prejudices began where the Southern man's ended, and there was a feeling bordering on rebellion in his heart and a sensation of nausea at the pit of his stomach as he gave his order to the negro waiter who came bowing and smiling, politeness personified, to receive it. . . . It was many weeks before he was able to eat what was set before him without thought of the color of the hands that served and prepared the food.[10]

The pattern the Klan followed was to first gain the support of the local Protestant ministers and then begin making public appearances. The method was repeated in Thebes in Alexander County at the Methodist Episcopal church, where the Reverend Charles L. Dawdy was holding a revival meeting in February 1924.[11] The house was filled to capacity, more than could be seated, when, at the beginning of the Sunday night services, "six Klansmen entered the church, marched past the altar and handed the pastor a letter containing a hundred dollar bill. The letter stated that seventy-five dollars were to be used for painting the church and twenty-five for the needs of the pastor."[12] The pastor's family was subsequently visited Thursday evening by a group of Thebes citizens who gave them a donation before the services. "This was the largest donation ever given to a pastor there," the Thebes newspaper correspondent reported.

The Congregational church in Mounds was crowded to capacity at its nightly service on Friday, April 11, 1924, when a "patriotic address" was given by the Reverend Lillian Britton Fulton of Jacksonville, Florida, who had been invited to conduct revival meetings. An ordained Congregational minister and Christian psychologist, Fulton had been well received in Mounds when she preached her "old-time religion" five months earlier.[13] Before she began to speak and while the congregation sang "The Battle Hymn of the Republic," representatives of the Ku Klux Klan silently marched down the aisle in their hoods and robes carrying American flags and took seats in the front of the assembly.[14] The stunt was planned and the seats reserved. After the song, the audience took their places in the pews and the Klan remained standing.

Local Klan organizer Forrest H. Moreland made a brief statement and then offered an envelope containing money to the pastor of the Congregational church, the Reverend George Burnside Waldron, a native of Marion County, Illinois. Moreland stated that the Klan was several hundred strong in Pulaski County, was 100 percent American, and stood for the enforcement of all laws. Waldron "thanked the Klan for the gift," which he gave to Mrs. Fulton, and "welcomed the Klan to come to the church often." He pledged the support of the church to any organization that worked for the betterment of Mounds and Pulaski County.

Forrest Moreland was prominent in Pulaski County and was successfully establishing the Ku Klux Klan in his two-county jurisdiction when he encountered resistance from Republican Pulaski County Sheriff Ira John Hudson, who proclaimed that the Ku Klux Klan would never be allowed to parade in their robes in his county. He seemed unable or unwilling to enforce the order, however. Hudson was a native of Hickman County, Kentucky, but spent most of his life in Pulaski County, where his family moved when he was a baby.[15] He graduated from Friendship School near Ullin at the age of 16, attended Southern Illinois Normal in Carbondale for two years, and was teaching school in Ullin by the age of 19. His 1918 draft registration stated Ira was "crippled" in the right hand. This disability did not prevent him from being elected four times as city clerk of Mounds and being elected sheriff in November 1922 at the age of 45. He was seen as a "local boy" and was popular in the county, but his influence was not enough to convince the Klan not to parade masked in the public streets of his county in defiance of his order.

Sheriff George Galligan of Williamson County had made the same declaration and arrested and jailed Jesse Earl Lashbrook of Harrisburg for wearing a mask in a parade in August 1924.[16] The warning from Sheriff Hudson, however, did not prevent the demonstration at the Congregational church in Mounds or other churches in the county, and Moreland boasted that there would have been more Klan members present at the Fulton meeting, but the size of the small church prevented it.[17]

The mayor of Mounds, Eustace Clifton Fletcher, a native of Dalton, Georgia, moved to the small town in Pulaski County from Chattanooga, Tennessee, with his family about 1902. He was supposed to have been present at the Congregational church that night to introduce Lillian Fulton. Perhaps he did not want the public association with the Klan or, as Waldron suggested, he "was too modest to face a great audience like this." Waldron notified the audience, however, that the mayor had taken it upon himself to order the Sunday closing of picture shows in Mounds beginning May 1. The news was met with cheers from the crowd in the church, many of whom credited the Klan for stopping the Sabbath-breaking moviegoers. The Mounds Town Council had refused to meet to discuss the issue, although they had been presented with a petition with more than five hundred signatures asking for the Sunday closings.

Eight Ku Klux Klan members followed established protocol and walked down the center aisle of the Methodist Episcopal Church in Ullin in Pulaski County on Thursday night, April 17, 1924. They were in their robes and presented the pastor, the Reverend Charles Luis Phifer, with a "small purse as an indication of their opinions of the Christian religion."[18] The leader asked if anyone wanted them to unmask or remove their hoods and no one spoke, so their identity remained secret. In defiance of Sheriff Hudson's order, before arriving at the church and after leaving the building, the Klan paraded through the streets of Ullin "without creating much excitement."

Other churches in Pulaski and Alexander Counties were visited by the Klan during the summer of 1924. The Sunday evening service of the Methodist Episcopal Church in Pulaski was interrupted by 13 robed Klansmen, and the minister was presented with an envelope containing money.[19] Fifty knights of the Klan also entered the night services of the Methodist church in Sandusky with fifty dollars to be used to hire a preacher in August 1924.[20] Oftentimes the Klan spokesman would hand the minister a letter to read like the one handed to the minister in Helena, Arkansas: "We who stand thus silently before you are more than a million strong; we are friends of this minister, this church, and this congregation; we stand for the Christian religion, for the protection of womanhood and for the everlasting supremacy of the White race. As such we most earnestly ask your friendship and your prayers."[21]

In southern Illinois, as in other places, the Ku Klux Klan was wed to Protestantism. The Reverend Charles D. McGehee, a Methodist minister from St. Louis, came to Cairo in October 1923 to speak before "a large assemblage" about the principal beliefs of the Klan.[22] McGehee was a "klockard," a paid lecturer who received twenty-five dollars for each speech.[23] He and fellow klockard the Reverend Dr. Cecil Clement Crawford, pastor of the Third Christian Church in St. Louis, spoke at the Cairo Opera House in January 1924 at a Klan meeting presided over by the Reverend Charles Leroy

Belknap, pastor of the Congregational church at Grand Chain.[24] Crawford was also editor of the *Patriot*, a publication of the Klan. This assembly was an open meeting attended mostly by members but also by those curious about the organization as well as some enemies of the Klan.

Crawford said the purpose of the Ku Klux Klan was to "develop 100 percent Americans." The term 100 Percent American meant White, Protestant, Anglo American, suggesting that all others were less American or even un-American. Strictly Protestant, White American rule would lead to better law enforcement, defeat of corrupt politicians, and protection of White womanhood and the home, he claimed.

Many Protestant churches in Pulaski and Alexander Counties opened their doors to Klan assemblies. There was another Klan meeting held at the Methodist Episcopal Church in Pulaski on Wednesday night, January 30, 1924, and it was "largely attended" by residents of Ullin and Pulaski.[25] The Reverend Harvey Beachum Atherton, a Baptist minister and farmer from Dongola and blind in his right eye, spoke, as did an unnamed Klan representative.

Another Ku Klux Klan meeting was held at the Baptist church in Ullin Sunday afternoon, March 31, 1924. "A big crowd was present and much comment was heard regarding the meeting for the order," the Ullin correspondent for the *Pulaski Enterprise* wrote in his column.[26] All the groundwork laid in the Baptist and Methodist churches in Ullin led to a large Klan initiation in the town. On Tuesday night, June 10, 1924, one thousand people witnessed a Ku Klux Klan meeting that was held in the pasture of Robert G. Carson's farm west of Ullin, just outside city limits.[27] Carson was a farmer and native of Vanderburgh County, Indiana, who moved to Ullin in 1910. A news release stated that cars were there from Grand Chain, Karnak, Cypress, Pulaski, Thebes, Elco, Tamms, Mounds, Wetaug, Dongola, and Cairo.

Most of those who participated in this first initiation held in Ullin were residents of that small town or from neighboring farms. The Reverend Thomas Benjamin "Ben" Sowers, pastor of the Methodist Episcopal church of West Frankfort, was the main speaker and was introduced by the Reverend Charles L. Phifer, pastor of the Ullin Methodist Episcopal church in Pulaski County and Beech Grove Methodist Episcopal church in Alexander County and an occasional preacher at New Hope Methodist Episcopal church near Ullin. Sowers was born near Ullin and was a former member of Beech Grove Methodist Episcopal church before entering the ministry. Phifer spoke about the "operations of the Klan in Ullin and vicinity." A large, 30-foot cross was burned, and the light from it could be seen for miles and was clearly visible from the west side of town populated by dozens of African American families.[28] The Klan's intended goal was to intimidate Black society as a whole and avoid carrying out acts of violence against individuals.[29]

The *Kloran*, also called the *White Book of the Ku Klux Klan*, guided Klan members in the initiation ceremony, or what they called "naturalization."[30] Prospective members first filled out a "petition of citizenship" and paid their klectoken to the "knight hawk," the person in charge of the candidates.[31] The ceremony bordered on the ridiculous, like many fraternal initiations, but was intended to be a very solemn occasion, and snickers would have been hushed. The knight hawk got permission to enter the klavern after the sign had been given and said that he had "important information and documents from the alien world for His Excellency."[32] The knight hawk read aloud from his *Kloran*, "Your Excellency: Sir, pursuant to my duty in seeking laudable adventure in the alien world, I found these men," and he stated the names of the men who were there to join the Klan. Then he said, "They having read the Imperial Proclamation of our Emperor, and prompted by unselfish motives, desire a nobler life. In consequence they have made the honorable decision to forsake the world of selfishness and fraternal alienation and emigrate to the delectable bounds of the Invisible Empire and become loyal citizens of the same."

The president of the local Klan, known as the exalted cyclops, then read aloud from the *Kloran*: "Faithful Night Hawk: This is indeed important information, and most pleasant to hear. Important, in that it evidences human progress; most pleasant, in that it reveals through you a klansman's sincere appreciation of his sacred mission among men and his fidelity to duty in the betterment of mankind. Their respective petitions will be received and justly considered."[33] If there were no objections to the men becoming members of the Klan, then the night hawk told the prospective members,

Worthy Aliens: His Excellency, the Exalted Cyclops, being the direct representative of His Majesty, our Emperor, and chief guardian of the portal of the Invisible Empire, has officially instructed me to inform you that it is the constant disposition of a klansman to assist those who aspire to things noble in thought and conduct and to extend a helping hand to the worthy. Therefore your desires are sincerely respected and your manly petitions are being seriously considered in the light of justice and honor. With true faith you may expect a just answer to your prayers, and your virtuous hopes will ultimately ripen into a sublime fruition. This is the decision of His Excellency, the Exalted Cyclops, with all his klan concurring.

Then the klokard (lecturer), the klaliff (vice president), and the kludd (chaplain) interrogated the "aliens" with the following questions to which they were to answer with an "emphatic 'Yes.'"

1. Is the motive prompting your ambition to be a klansman serious and unselfish?
2. Are you a native-born white, Gentile American citizen?
3. Are you absolutely opposed to and free of any allegiance of any nature to any cause, government, people, sect or ruler that is foreign to the United States of America?
4. Do you believe in the tenets of the Christian religion?
5. Do you esteem the United States of America and its institutions above any other government, civil, political or ecclesiastical, in the whole world?
6. Will you, without mental reservation, take a solemn oath to defend, preserve and enforce same?
7. Do you believe in clannishness and will you faithfully practice same towards klansmen?
8. Do you believe in and will you faithfully strive for the eternal maintenance of white supremacy?
9. Will you faithfully obey our constitution and laws, and conform willingly to all our usages, requirement and regulations?
10. Can you be always depended on?

After being initiated, the "brothers" raised their front aprons to reveal their faces. Once organized, each klavern elected 12 officers. Membership lists were confidential and minutes of klavern meetings are rare. No local records are known to exist in Pulaski or Alexander County.

The work done in churches in Alexander County also proved successful to the Klan. More than a thousand people assembled at a similar initiation meeting in Thebes on Sunday, June 15, 1924, where the meeting started in the afternoon and continued into the evening.[34] Twenty-five men were sworn in to the Invisible Empire by the former Illinois Grand Titan Charles McGehee, whose East St. Louis klavern membership reportedly peaked at eight thousand in 1925.[35] Another meeting was planned in Elco on June 19, and a huge gathering was announced for July 4 near Cairo.

McGehee was a Klan leader and former pastor of Stewards Haven Street Methodist Episcopal Church, South, in Carondelet, Missouri.[36] When a newspaper report was read in March 1923 by Bishop William Fletcher McMurry stating that McGehee planned to deliver a sermon titled "The Principles of the Ku Klux Klan," he telegrammed the pastor forbidding the sermon. McMurry wrote McGehee on March 8, 1923, advising him that he had a right as an individual to be a member of the Klan but that he "cannot use his position as pastor to take advantage of access to the people to become a spokesman for any institution other than the church" and stated that McGehee's recruiting activities were causing division within his church.[37] McGehee obeyed the order but enlisted the help of his mother after he was forbidden to speak.[38] On the night he was to speak, the church was crowded to capacity with about eight hundred men and women, and he stated, "As a loyal Methodist preacher and a loyal Klansman I obey the law of the church."[39] He then introduced his mother, who McMurry claimed "was running the women of the Ku Klux Klan," and she delivered the message that night.[40]

After McGehee was appointed as chaplain and first lieutenant of the United States Army Reserve Corps in 1923, the American Legion Post in St. Louis passed a resolution stating that McGehee was "unfit to minister to soldiers," and he was removed in March 1923 because he was not a clergyman in good standing.[41] Charges against him stated that he "has displayed the most violent feeling against certain creeds and races and has fostered racial strife and hatred."[42] McGehee was subsequently praised in the *Fiery Cross*, a Klan newspaper published in Indianapolis, in April 1923 for his "unmitigated courage" for preaching an "extraordinary expression of Christian grace and 100 percent Americanism" from his pulpit.[43]

McGehee met with Bishop McMurry on August 31, 1923, at his office in St. Louis, but later claimed McMurry struck him in the mouth with his fist. He filed charges against the bishop for assault but later dropped the suit. At a St. Louis Conference church trial, McGehee was accused of "immorality, namely falsehood and bearing false witness." Several eyewitnesses were called who contradicted McGehee's claim of assault, and McGehee was not only defrocked but expelled from membership in the church in October 1923.[44] Two months later, he lost an appeal to the Methodist Episcopal Church,

South leaders at Nashville, Tennessee.[45] He then tried to join the ministry of the Presbyterian church, but the Illinois Synod refused him and he devoted his time to Klan recruitment.[46] In a statement made to the church court when he appealed his case, he said, "You will not keep me from preaching. I preach every night, in the cities throughout Illinois: Monday in Marion and Herrin and others. I mention that to let you know I am still preaching and preaching not to divide Protestantism, but to unite it. . . . If it comes to a choice between the Methodist Church and the Klan, then I shall choose the Klan."[47]

By January 1924, McGehee was living in Cairo and was involved in local recruitment efforts and in planning events. A July 4 picnic in 1924 held at Roth's Crossing, about five miles north of Cairo, attracted some seven thousand people.[48] A Carbondale newspaper reported that hundreds of automobiles passed through that town on the way to Cairo.[49] Attendees poured into Illinois's southernmost town from three states. A parade of robed and hooded Klansmen started down Sycamore Street in Cairo at the same time a baseball game ended, and the *Cairo Evening Citizen* reported it was impossible to tell how many cars were in the parade and how many autos were caught in the traffic. Regardless, there was a major initiation in the afternoon, with speakers before and after the ceremony and fireworks that night.

Many were attracted to the Klan because of its alleged financial support to local Protestant churches, its message of Protestant morality, and its "law enforcement." The Klan stressed Protestant morality when trying to recruit members, but it had White supremacy as its foundation. The Klan encouraged fear of Americans of African descent, Jews, "non-Nordic" immigrants, and Catholics. The old argument that aliens were taking jobs from White Protestant Americans was used. Being Catholic was incompatible with being a true American, they said, for Catholics owed their allegiance to a foreign pope.

At the height of the Klan's success in Alexander and Pulaski Counties, Chicago's Ida B. Wells-Barnett returned to Cairo in March 1924. A civil rights leader and one of the founders of the National Association for the Advancement of Colored People, she is best known for her campaign against lynching. This was her second trip to Cairo, as she came in 1909 (at the request of her husband, who worked in the Cook County State's attorney's office in Chicago) to investigate the lynching of Will "Froggie" James.[50] During her second visit to Cairo, on March 17, 1924, she spoke at Sumner High School at 8 P.M.[51] She came at the invitation of the Yates Woman's Club of Cairo and "brought a special message to women."[52] The *Citizen* provided no further details about what she said, only stating that Miss Payne, president of the local club, presided at the meeting and that Eugene White provided music.

On the same night Wells-Barnett was to speak in Cairo, a news article advertised an informational meeting in Mound City sponsored by the Ku Klux Klan. The Reverend Philip Rutherford Glotfelty of the Methodist Episcopal church in Herrin, and the Reverend Alfred Mitchell Stickney, pastor of the Southern Methodist Episcopal church in Marion, spoke at the Congregational church in Mound City.[53] Stickney had pastored the church at Grand Tower in Jackson County in 1920 and was chairman of the Marion Ministerial Association. Glotfelty was first publicly visited by 20 members of the Klan at his church in June 1923, and he became the leader of the Herrin Klan. The two ministers were invited to Mound City by the Pulaski County Ministerial Association and claimed they were going to tell listeners the "truth about Williamson."[54] The Pulaski County Ministerial Association had been formed in January 1924 "to further the work of churches of the county in usefulness, both to the religious cause and social cause" but immediately faced controversy because "colored ministers were kept out."[55]

Glotfelty spoke about the bootleggers and corrupt politicians in Williamson County and never mentioned the Klan by name. He claimed that "decent citizens" were laughed at when they met with county and state officials to discuss the disregard for law in Williamson County, especially in regard to enforcement of Prohibition. Indeed, Governor Small told one representative, with a laugh, "You get what you elect."[56] The preacher said their last hope for cleaning up Williamson County was in Washington, D.C., and representatives from the county went to meet with Prohibition Commissioner Roy Asa Haynes, who promised support. More importantly, it was there that the Williamson County citizens first met Glenn Young, who came back with them to lead the Klan's efforts to enforce Prohibition in the region. To "clean up" Pulaski County and shut down bootleggers there, Glotfelty suggested they should follow the example of Williamson and look to the Klan to lead the way.

There was communication and cooperation between the Klan in Williamson County and that in Pulaski County. In fact, when a barbecue and "open air meeting" of the Ku Klux Klan was held at Herrin, about two hundred people from Pulaski County attended.[57] Many also attended the Belleville picnic and barbecue on Memorial Day, even though its city council objected to the rally in their town. It was expected that one hundred thousand Klan members and supporters would be at Belleville, according to an Associated Press news release.[58] By this time, former Carondelet minister Charles McGehee was making his living as an insurance salesman in East St. Louis and was the "Great Titan of Province No. 1, Realm of Illinois," headquartered at Centralia. The Belleville City Council unanimously adopted a resolution instructing Mayor Joseph J. Anton to use the police force to "prevent and suppress the holding of a Ku Klux Klan parade and picnic," but the event went on as planned. The city council feared trouble as Klan leader Young had been shot and injured during an ambush on May 23, just a week before Memorial Day, during the Klan War in Williamson and Franklin Counties.

Klan activity led to an escalation of violence. McGehee had been the main speaker at a Klan meeting held in April 1924, in Raleigh in Saline County, about four miles north of Harrisburg.[59] Afterward, the gathering assembled in an open field, where several hundred candidates were welcomed into the Klan. This first meeting of the year in Saline County attracted fifteen thousand persons according to newspaper accounts, although that number was likely exaggerated. A few weeks after the meeting, on May 4, a lynching was attempted at Harrisburg by about a hundred men who swarmed the county jail.[60] They planned to hang Norman Keys, a Black man who had reportedly confessed to attacking Cal Lewis, an aged White businessman, during an attempted robbery of his store in Harrisburg. Sheriff John Small, anticipating a lynch mob, moved Keys from the jail to an undisclosed location and averted a lynching. The Klan had not officially encouraged or condoned the attempted lynching, but it seems likely that there were Klansmen and Klan supporters in the lynch mob. When the Klan spewed words of White supremacy and fear of African American men and a need to control them, it is not surprising that such rhetoric would follow its course toward violence.

In Cairo, the county seat of Alexander County, there is no record of violence against Americans of African descent by the newly organized Klan, but it did cause disruption in one Black church. The Reverend Lewine Arthur Weaver, pastor of Mount Moriah Baptist Church at Twenty-Seventh and Poplar, was accused by some members of sympathizing with the Ku Klux Klan and allowing members of the Klan to use the basement of the church to dress in their regalia before a meeting in the town.[61] Although the Klan was vehemently racist in its rhetoric, it claimed it wanted to promote Protestant Christianity among African Americans. On rare occasions they even marched robed into religious services and made donations to African American churches, as the Klan did in Oneida, New York; Trenton, New Jersey; and Texas in 1924.[62] Weaver mentioned the allegations against him in a church meeting, and church members Robert Wilkins and Merriam Willis stood and said if the charges were true Weaver should be censured. An argument between the three men escalated, and Weaver picked up a chair to strike Willis, and when Wilkins intervened, Weaver struck him in the jaw with his fist. Wilkins pressed charges; Weaver pleaded guilty and soon left Cairo to accept a position as pastor of Mt. Zion Baptist Church in Peoria, Illinois.[63]

An examination of the 1923 and 1924 newspaper headlines in Pulaski and Alexander Counties from the time the Klan was organizing in the area shows that the local media had continued to encourage and support much of the fear of Americans of African descent. Headlines included, "Seek Negro Who Murdered a Policeman,"[64] "Negro Admits to Eight Deaths, Other Crimes,"[65] "One Killed, Seven Hurt, as Negro Cuts,"[66] "Crippled White Man Attacked by Negro,"[67] "Negro Sent Up 21 Years for Murder,"[68] "Negress Denies Giving Poison to Children,"[69] "Negro Shoots Youth Then Attacks Girl,"[70] "Negro Held for Assault to Kill,"[71] "Olmsted Boy Is Killed by Negro,"[72] and "Escaped Negro Murderer Caught near Sandusky."[73]

Americans of African descent were the most threatened and the most vocal in opposing the Klan. With the popularity of the Ku Klux Klan growing in Pulaski County, it is not surprising that the 1915 silent movie *The Birth of a Nation* was brought to the Palm Theater in Mound City for a scheduled three-day run in February 1925.[74] As with earlier stage productions in Cairo in the early 1900s, there was objection to showing the film.

Influential African American leaders in Pulaski County lodged a formal complaint with Mound City Mayor Beverly Leonard Hendrix. Unlike the protest lodged in Cairo almost 20 years earlier to the performance of *The Clansman*, this one was successful, and the mayor issued an order refusing to allow the movie to be shown. The movie, some local Black leaders believed, was overtly racist, but two scenes in particular were offensive. In one scene, a White girl commits suicide by leaping from a cliff in order to escape a Black male pursuer, and in another, a non-White politician tries to force a White man to allow him to marry his daughter. The movie was shown as scheduled in Anna in Union County, and many from Mound City went there to see it.

Most Americans of African descent realized the threat posed by the growing local membership in the Ku Klux Klan, but other groups in Alexander and Pulaski Counties were also targeted. In the minds of Klansmen, Jews, who were banned from joining the organization, were the enemy of America and the spreaders of Bolshevism or communism, who could not fully assimilate into American society or demonstrate patriotism or loyalty to any country: "A Jew is a Jew and never a White American."[75] Few members paused to realize that Jesus would not be allowed to join the Klan if he returned.

Orthodox Jews had met in Cairo since the Civil War, but Montefiore Reformed Jewish Congregation was organized there in 1894 by Rabbi Bernard Sadler.[76] Most members in the 1920s were recent immigrants from Europe or their American-born children.[77] As Reformed Jews, they emphasized what they had in common with their non-Jewish neighbors and tried integrating into the dominant White American society. They held services on Friday nights and Sundays so that members could conduct business on Saturdays, the traditional Jewish Sabbath, and rather than bar mitzvahs or bat mitzvahs they held confirmations. They also allowed men and women to sit together at services, and wearing of yarmulkes was optional. At the time the Klan was organizing in Alexander and Pulaski Counties, the Montefiore Congregation numbered about a hundred, mostly from merchant families living in Cairo and Mound City. The local Ku Klux Klan may have boycotted Jewish-owned businesses, but the anti-Semitic rhetoric of the national Klan organization was not stressed in Alexander and Pulaski Counties. In fact, no anti-Semitic propaganda is found in extant issues of newspapers published in the counties. Rabbi Sadler frequently submitted articles to the *Cairo Bulletin* explaining the history and significance of Jewish holidays and traditions and invited Christians to attend his services. Jewish businesses in Cairo were also among the newspaper's largest advertisers, and activities and services of Montefiore Synagogue were listed in the Sunday edition in the column "Today at Cairo Churches."

Catholics were also viewed as un-American by the Ku Klux Klan but resided in Alexander and Pulaski Counties by the hundreds. There were two Catholic churches in Cairo: St. Patrick's, founded in 1838 mainly by Irish immigrants, and St. Joseph's, established by Germans in 1870. In Pulaski County, Catholic churches included St. Catherine of Alexandria in Grand Chain, the Church of the Immaculate Conception St. Mary in Mound City, St. Raphael's in Mounds, and St. Joseph Church in Wetaug. In fact, Wetaug had been the home of a Benedictine Monastery from 1881 to 1904, when the monks closed it and moved to Canada.

Catholics in the area supported St. Joseph's parochial school in Cairo, which was staffed by nuns from Loretto Convent, and St. Patrick's Roman Catholic Church conducted a school in the church basement. St. Catherine's in Grand Chain also conducted a school, and from 1922 to 1925 high school courses were offered. St. Mary's Infirmary, where the nursing staff comprised Catholic nuns, attracted patients of diverse religious beliefs to the city from the tristate region and was a landmark that citizens of all religions appreciated. As with anti-Semitism, there is no evidence that the anti-Catholicism of the Klan was stressed locally.

Many of those who joined the Klan klaverns organized in Pulaski and Alexander Counties knew and interacted to a limited degree with Catholics, and many of them had likely shopped in Jewish-owned stores in Cairo and Mound City. Protestant children attended public school with Jewish children and some Catholic children. Although they were not seen in Protestant churches on Sunday mornings, Catholics and Jews were seen by Protestants as neighbors and maybe even friends. The color line between White Protestants and Americans of African descent, however, was much more strictly drawn and was seldom crossed. Schools and churches were segregated, and contact between Blacks and Whites was discouraged except in politics. It was more difficult for the Klan to convince local members that Jews and Catholics were a threat, but suspicion and fear of African Americans were present among many White residents long before the Klan made its appearance. These deep-seated concerns, as well as the racism of man, were what attracted people to the Ku Klux Klan. Americans of African descent were viewed as a threat, and the Klan promised to provide the means to control them.

Matinee and Night, Saturday, April 21st

The Most Astounding Success of the Century

The Ku=Klux Klan

A Drama of Absorbing Interest dealing with the "Invisible Empire" which in 1870 stamped out Negro Rule in the South : : : :

A Direct Contradiction of Uncle Tom's Cabin

PRICES: Matinee 25 and 50c. Night—Last three rows of lower floor 57c; Balance $1.00; Dress Circle 50c; Gallery 25c. Seats on sale at Opera House Box Office, Friday, April 20th, at 8:30 A. M.

The performance of *The Ku Klux Klan* in April 1906 was advertised in the local newspapers. *Cairo Evening Citizen*, April 16, 1906.

The Cairo Opera House was the site of a 1904 lecture by the Reverend Thomas F. Dixon, author of the Klan trilogy; a 1906 performance of the play *The Ku Klux Klan*; and a 1924 Klan meeting. *Cairo Illustrated*, c. 1910.

The costume worn by the southern Illinois Ku Klux Klan was similar to that of the Southern Klan. *St. Louis Republican*, August 23, 1875.

The Congregational church in Mounds was filled to capacity when local Ku Klux Klan members visited during a revival service on Friday, April 11, 1924. Postcard from the collection of Darrel Dexter.

Ira J. Hudson was sheriff of Pulaski County during the years of Klan recruitment in the region. From *History of Pulaski County*.

Form K-115

APPLICATION FOR CITIZENSHIP
IN THE
INVISIBLE EMPIRE
KNIGHTS OF THE KU KLUX KLAN
(INCORPORATED)

To His Majesty the Imperial Wizard, Emperor of the Invisible Empire, Knights of the Ku Klux Klan:

I, the undersigned, a native born, true and loyal citizen of the United States of America, being a white male Gentile person of temperate habits, sound in mind and a believer in the tenets of the Christian religion, the maintenance of White Supremacy and the principles of a "pure Americanism," do most respectfully apply for membership in the Knights of the Ku Klux Klan through

Klan No............................, Realm of...

I guarantee on my honor to conform strictly to all rules and requirements regulating my "naturalization" and the continuance of my membership, and at all times a strict and loyal obedience to your constitutional authority and the constitution and laws of the fraternity, not in conflict with the constitution and constitutional laws of the United States of America and the states thereof. If I prove untrue as a Klansman I will willingly accept as my portion whatever penalty your authority may impose.

The required "klectokon" accompanies this application.

Signed...Applicant

Endorsed by   Residence Address ....

Kl...   Business Address ....

Kl...   Date...192......

The person securing this application must sign on top line above. NOTICE—Check the Address to which mail may be sent.

NOTICE

The sum of this donation MUST accompany application, if possible. Upon payment of same by applicant this certificate is made out and signed by person securing application, then detached and given to applicant, who will keep same and bring it with him when he is called, and then turn it in on demand in lieu of the cash.

DO NOT detach if donation is not paid in advance.

OFFICIAL CERTIFICATE OF DONATION

This certifies that...

has donated the sum of TEN DOLLARS to the propagating fund of the

KNIGHTS OF THE KU KLUX KLAN (Inc.)

and same is accepted as such and as full sum of *"KLECTOKON"* entitling him to be received, on the acceptance of his application, under the laws, regulations and requirements of the Order, duly naturalized and to have and to hold all the rights, titles, honors and protection as a citizen of the Invisible Empire. He enters through the portal of

Klan No..............., Realm of..........................

Date.., 192......

Received in trust for the
KNIGHTS OF THE KU KLUX KLAN, (INC.)

By Kl...

A signed application, endorsed by two Klan members, was the initial step to become a Klansman. Courtesy of Southern Illinois Special Collections Research Center, Morris Library, Carbondale.

The Carson pasture west of Ullin was the site of a large Klan initiation, or "naturalization," ceremony in 1924. Photo by Darrel Dexter.

INVISIBLE EMPIRE

K-UNO   K-DUO

KNIGHTS OF THE KU KLUX KLAN

HONOR

This certifies that

the bearer, K.L._____whose signature
appears on the reverse side hereof, has been found
loyal and worthy of advancement in the mysteries of ~ ~ ~

Klankraft

and has been passed to K-Duo, or Knights Kamellia, and is
entitled to all the rights and privileges thereof. This
certificate also entitles the bearer to all the rights and
privileges of a Klansman of K-Uno. In witness whereof I
have hereunto affixed my signature and the seal of my Klan.

Signed _____

VOID AFTER_____   KLIGRAPP
                                    KNO_____Realm _____

Once accepted into the Invisible Empire of the Knights of the Ku Klux
Klan, a membership card was issued. Courtesy of Southern Illinois Special
Collections Research Center, Morris Library, Carbondale.

Klansmen could be summoned to special meetings at any time. Courtesy of Southern Illinois Special Collections Research Center, Carbondale.

Ida B. Wells-Barnett made her second visit to Cairo during the height of Klan recruitment in the region. Chicago History Museum.

St. Mary's Catholic Church in Mound City was one of six Catholic churches in Pulaski and Alexander Counties in 1924 and was organized before the Civil War. Postcard from the collection of Darrel Dexter.

St. Joseph's School in Cairo was staffed by the sisters of Loretto Convent in the town. Postcard from the collection of Darrel Dexter.

Daisy Wilson was an active, outdoors-loving farm girl before her murder in 1924. Photo courtesy of the Mahoney family.

Daisy Wilson and her father, James C. Wilson, on the right, are pictured sitting on the front steps of the Wilson farmhouse near Villa Ridge. The first woman from the left was Daisy's cousin, Bertha Gladys Deimund, of Cairo, and the second an unidentified friend. Photo courtesy of the Mahoney family.

The Illinois Central Railroad yard in Mounds was the location of the apprehension of two men accused of the murder of Daisy Wilson in 1924. Postcard from the collection of Darrel Dexter.

An angry lynch mob surrounded the Pulaski County Courthouse and jail in 1924 intent on killing the two men arrested for the murder of Daisy Wilson. Postcard from collection of Darrel Dexter.

Ida B. Wells-Barnett spoke at Sumner High School in Cairo during the height of Klan recruitment in Pulaski and Alexander Counties. *Cairo Illustrated*, 1903.

CHAPTER SIX

The Elco Trouble

꙰

AS THE KLAN WAS INCREASING its organization efforts in
Alexander and Pulaski Counties, two incidents occurred that reveal how strong the sentiment against Americans of African descent was among some of the rural White citizens and the degree of violence
and intimidation they were willing to use to control them. New Hope was a
rural farming settlement southeast of Ullin, and "no colored folks tolerated" was the predominant motto of the residents. Several visited a "colored man" and his family who had recently moved from Charleston,
Missouri, recruited by a White farmer to help raise cotton. They placed a
bundle of switches on his porch with a note attached that explained that
January 11, 1924, one week from the day of their visit, was the date affixed by
them for his family's removal. The man was not in a position to safely resist
and spent the next day locating a new place to live.[1]

The reaction to a similar incident in the Elco area of Alexander County
only six miles away and just a few days later was much different. Elco was only
a small village along the Mobile and Ohio Railroad in 1924 with fewer than
one hundred residents. There were less than two hundred dwellings in all of
Elco Precinct, and the 1920 census counted only 915 people, the vast majority of them scattered on small farms. Some of the families had lived in the
area for nearly a hundred years, and generations of intermarriage among
neighbors created strong family ties among them.

A group of White men visited the tenant house on the farm of Israel Cauble between Elco and Tamms in the early morning hours of Wednesday, January 9, 1924. Some of the men carried containers of kerosene, intending to
burn the house and force the Black families living there to flee. From the front
yard they called the "negro spokesman," Dan Smothers, out of the house and
told him that he and the others had to leave.[2] They were the first African

Americans in Alexander County who dared to live in the area north of the "dead line," where Black people were not allowed to reside. It was a well-known but unwritten rule that Americans of African descent were not allowed to reside north of the gravel pit switch track of the Mobile and Ohio Railroad north of Tamms in Alexander County.

After the talk, Smothers went back inside the house after inviting the White men in for further discussion. When the White guardians of segregation discovered that four of the eight men inside were armed with high-powered rifles and willing to defend themselves, they abandoned their cans of kerosene and plans to burn the house, at least for that night. The disgruntled men lingered outside for a few more minutes discussing their dilemma and then left through the front gate, firing their guns into the house as they retreated. The gunfire was returned and some one hundred shots were exchanged, but none of the White men were hit.[3]

Inside, Dan Smothers was shot in the arm during the melee, and before sunrise a doctor (probably one of the two physicians living in Tamms) arrived to dress his wound.[4] The doctor offered to go inside to examine Smothers, but no one in the house would light a lamp for him because they thought it was a trick, afraid the house was still being watched by men with guns.[5] The doctor was too frightened to go inside the dark house, so he left before examining the man's gunshot wound.

When news of the gunfight reached Cairo, Alexander County Sheriff James S. Roche and his son, Deputy Leslie B. Roche, went to Elco after sunrise to investigate. The Roches found the wounded man inside and the unused kerosene and other flammable material in containers lying in front of the house. Late in the afternoon, they brought Smothers back to Cairo for treatment at St. Mary's Hospital, which had a segregated ward for African American patients. His physical injuries were initially reported in a Cairo newspaper to be minor, but Smothers spent 18 days in the hospital.[6] All that the inhabitants of the house could tell the law officers was that they had been attacked by a group of White men who were strangers to them. (Smothers later identified Deputy Sheriff John Brown as the leader in the attack.)[7] Sheriff Roche warned the citizens through the local press that "such disturbances between whites and blacks must stop," but he fell short of placing the blame on the White attackers. Roche was an elected official and, as a Republican, needed the vote of Americans of African descent to remain in office, but he did not want to alienate rural White voters.[8] It was a delicate balancing act that Republican politicians in Alexander and Pulaski Counties had to learn if they wanted to remain in office.

The families living in the tenant house were not voters but recent arrivals from the South and had come to work for Israel Cauble to plant several hundred acres of cotton when spring arrived.[9] Black migrant laborers were sometimes brought to the county at harvest time to pick cotton for the few farmers who grew it, but Cauble was breaking precedent by settling them in a more permanent fashion upon his farm for the entire growing season.

The precedent occurred 50 years earlier, during the Civil War, when Benjamin Fenton erected a cotton gin on his farm west of Jonesboro, just fifteen miles north of Elco, and tried to bring 40 African American laborers from contraband camps in Cairo to plant four hundred acres in cotton.[10] News of his plan reached the people around Anna and Jonesboro, and in April 1863, a mob of about 25 armed men met the workers and their small military escort at the Union-Alexander county line, just north of Elco, and forced Fenton to send them back to Cairo.[11] Their objection was not to the cultivation of cotton but to the "introduction of colored laborers."[12]

The violence was repeated two years later when Fenton again brought 18 Black workers to the county to pick cotton. This time "a mob composed of the meanest and lowest class of citizens" disguised and armed themselves and went at night to where the workers were camped next to the cotton gin. They fired into the gin and the camp and notified Fenton the workers must leave.[13] Eight of the workers were frightened away. A Cairo newspaper reported Fenton said he would "meet the scoundrels with force," and Lt. Sweeney of the Freedman's Bureau at Cairo came to aid in protecting the workers. While soldiers were present, peace prevailed, but the workers advised Sweeney that when the "blue coats" left they would soon follow.[14]

For many decades following the Civil War, hundreds of African Americans living in Cairo became migrant farm workers, heading south to pick cotton in the fall of each year.[15] Beginning in September, planters from southern states arrived in Cairo to recruit workers to labor in the cotton fields during harvest. Hundreds of men, women, and children camped out on the levees awaiting the arrival of steamboats to take them south.[16] In 1914, farmers in Hickman, Kentucky, sent out a request to Cairo for three hundred cotton pickers, ironically only six years after notices were posted in Hickman warning the entire Black population to leave or face violence.[17] They also sent word to St. Louis, Missouri, asking the police there to "send down all men who apply at the station for work."[18] The police station was not an unemployment office, but vagrancy laws allowed policemen to arrest anyone they chose to detain who was in the city without money and unemployed.

Just as coming north to plant cotton in southern Illinois could be precarious, going south to work as laborers during cotton season was not without its dangers. A farmer named Kennedy who had three hundred acres in Ballard County, Kentucky, hired Black workers from Olmsted in Pulaski County to work on his farm. In March 1904, he was awakened by noise coming from his barn and, leaving his bed to investigate, discovered a group of six "white cappers," who warned him to stop hiring Black laborers from Illinois or they would return and burn his barn. The *Paducah News-Democrat* reported the incident and stated, "These Illinois negroes are not as respectful as their Kentucky brethren, and it appears that Mr. Kennedy's action has enraged some of his neighbors."[19]

Racial violence could be found in the entire region. Across the Ohio River from Mound City, in LaCenter, Kentucky, African American residents were notified in July 1904 to leave within 48 hours. In this instance, some leading White citizens stepped forward to offer their support and pledged that they would protect the families to the full extent of the law.[20] Despite their promises, on August 1, 1904, a loud explosion awakened the residents of LaCenter. Dynamite had been placed under the cabin occupied by the African American workers. Fortunately no one was injured and slight damage was done to the building.[21]

The sentiment was the same in southeast Missouri. When a Cairo man, Clarence J. DeLaney, hired six Americans of African descent as laborers to work in a saw mill at Henderson's Mound in New Madrid County in September 1905, it led to what newspaper accounts called a "race war." On the night of September 13 the camp was visited by a group of about 20 White residents of the Missouri Bootheel, who had threatened violence if he hired Black workers. They fired about 75 shots into his bedroom where his wife was asleep. DeLaney was injured, being slightly grazed by a bullet on his knuckles. He raised the American flag, refused to fire his workers, and offered to arm them with rifles to defend themselves and their jobs.[22] The frightened workers declined to stay and fight and left the county, no doubt believing they were not being paid enough to fight for the right to work there.[23]

The agricultural sector had problems in addition to finding workers. Although some businesses and industries benefitted from prosperous years during the Roaring Twenties, farmers faced tough economic times. New machinery was expensive, while prices for grain and other farm produce fell, in part due to surpluses as Europe returned to growing its own food after World War I. The Great Depression started for farmers in the 1920s, and those in southern Illinois needed to diversify their crops from the staples corn and wheat to include a cash crop. The boll weevil had decimated southern cotton fields in the 1920s, but the pests had not reached southern Illinois, where earlier frosts had killed the insect. Some farmers saw an economic opportunity by turning their grain fields into cotton fields, just as farmers had done during the Civil War. The Alexander County National Bank in Cairo had produced a small booklet, *Cotton in Southern Illinois* by Dr. L. T. Fox of Mississippi, which they distributed to local farmers free of charge.[24] It offered advice on producing, ginning, and marketing cotton.

The first year cotton began to be grown on a large scale for market in Pulaski or Alexander County since the Civil War was 1923, when bottom land near the Mississippi River in Union and Alexander Counties was planted in cotton and proved "successful beyond the most sanguine expectations."[25] The *Pulaski Enterprise* reported in February 1923 that a few "colored growers" had migrated to Pulaski County in search of land to rent so they could grow cotton.[26] Three hundred cotton farmers attended a meeting at the Pulaski County Courthouse, where experts answered questions, and it was optimistically predicted that the cotton crop in Alexander and Pulaski Counties would total $2 million with twelve thousand acres planted.[27] Initial reports for the 1923 cotton crop were encouraging, and 25 Pulaski County cotton farmers organized a cooperative in July 1924 to sell their product collectively at a better price after cotton picking season arrived in the fall.[28] Enthusiasm for the crop continued to grow, and in Mound City, two cotton gins were erected in 1924.[29] Interest was strong throughout southern Illinois for cotton production, but in parts of Pulaski, Alexander, and Union Counties there was strong opposition to the presence of Black workers.

Several hundred African American agricultural workers were recruited to plant cotton, mostly in Union County.[30] At Ware, a cotton gin was erected that could produce 35 bales of cotton every 10 hours.[31] Some landowners, such as Hervey Adelbert "H. A." DuBois and Thomas Arthur "T. A." DuBois, brothers and Cobden merchants, proceeded with cotton production with Black laborers on their land in the Mississippi Bottoms, despite the known opposition to Black residency there. After the DuBois brothers received threatening letters for daring to encourage the residency of Americans of African descent in Union County, the two men placed an advertisement in the February 8, 1924, *Jonesboro Gazette*, a weekly newspaper in Union County: "$100.00 for information that will lead to the arrest and conviction of the party or parties who posted warning signs in front of houses occupied by our colored people near Wolf Lake. . . . $200.00 for information that will lead to the arrest and conviction of the parties who wrote letters to each of us threatening our lives. This $200.00 will apply separately to each letter, one to H.A. and the other to T.A. DuBois.[32]

By referring to the occupants of their tenant houses as "our colored people," the DuBois brothers may have been expressing a racist paternalistic view, or perhaps they thought that by identifying them as "our colored people" they could extend some level of protection to their employees. Any offense against Black workers near Wolf Lake was now an offense against two prominent White merchants whose lives had also been threatened.

The *Jonesboro Gazette* ran the advertisement but reassured the DuBois brothers and its other readers that the frightful disregard for the law experienced near Elco in Alexander County would not be repeated in Union County: "It is inconceivable that any overt acts of lawlessness will follow these threats. Mob law will not be tolerated in Union County, and if there is any latent spirit of lawlessness like that hinted at in the anonymous letters, it should be promptly met and sternly repressed, and to this end the land owners and the negroes will have the full power of the constituted authorities and of all law abiding citizens back of them."

The editor of the *Jonesboro Gazette* had a short memory, as lawlessness had certainly been tolerated in Union County in 1863 when Benjamin Fenton tried locating African Americans there to plant cotton. In November 1909, 10 Black men who worked at the rock quarry about a mile east of Anna received advance notice that a group of White men were marching to the quarry to force them to leave, and they only avoided violence by escaping to the woods and not returning.[33] A year later, in 1910, a Black employee working as a hostler in Anna for the owner of the *Anna Democrat* was threatened with dynamite if he did not leave Anna.[34]

Thus, Israel Cauble was not the first to contemplate using imported Black labor. Darrell James, another Elco farmer, owned four hundred acres he wanted to plant in cotton, but he "found it inadvisable to attempt to do so because of the strong feeling in the neighborhood against negroes" and decided to put his land in sheep pasturage and corn.[35] He claimed in an interview with the *Cairo Bulletin* that most people were opposed to Americans of African descent settling in Alexander County north of the gravel pit switch track of the Mobile and Ohio Railroad, which is what led to the attack on the Cauble tenant house north of that line.

James did not believe cotton could be grown on a large scale without Black laborers because he believed Whites were unfamiliar with how to tend the crop and would not work at "reasonable wages," and because he believed "too many negroes would steal and were otherwise undesirable neighbors, although admitting there were many good people among them."[36]

Unlike the incident at New Hope, the problems in Elco did not disappear after the first attack on the house in January 1924. A house on the Cauble farm was burned on Monday, January 28, and the same house that had earlier been attacked was dynamited the following night. A stick of dynamite thrown at the tenant house by a man riding a mule exploded and damaged a part of the front porch.[37] No one was injured and the attacker continued on the dirt road on the back of his mule toward Elco.

Israel Cauble decided to fight. A 62-year-old farmer and storekeeper in Elco, he had served as county commissioner and was a Republican candidate for sheriff in 1914.[38] He had lived in Alexander County his entire life and was born a few months before his father, Miles Cauble, left home to serve as a Union soldier in the Civil War. Israel still lived on the family farm with his wife, Mary (Vick) Cauble, and a brother, Joshua Miles Cauble. Israel and Mary's only child, Bessie Gertrude, had left home four years earlier when she married Alfred White, a train car repairer for the Mobile and Ohio Railroad in Tamms.

Cauble's reputation in the community was not all positive. He had been accused of fathering a child by Dora (Thompson) Beasley, the wife of William R. Beasley, who had been paralyzed in a railroad accident, and of giving her three dollars to get an abortion from Dr. Luther F. Robinson at Ullin. Dora died October 23, 1904, from the effects of the operation, but two days earlier had told her sister her secrets.[39] Also damaging to Cauble's status was the report in the county newspapers of his assault against his 74-year-old great-aunt, Sophia Malinda (Cauble) Hartline. Mrs. Hartline, who kept a hotel at Elco, claimed she had asked Cauble to keep his horses out of her meadow and he "pushed her violently to the ground causing her bodily injury."[40] Deputy Sheriff William White arrested Cauble and took him to Cairo, where he was tried before Justice of the Peace Andrew J. Ross, fined ten dollars and cost, and released after paying the court twenty-six dollars.[41] One can only speculate whether animosity lingered among residents against Israel Cauble for what had happened decades earlier and whether that contributed to the Elco Trouble.

Cauble repaired the dynamite damage to the tenant house, and the families living there continued to occupy it. In defiance, he even erected more tenant houses on his farm and announced that he planned to plant all of his land in cotton and bring in Black families from the South to tend the crops. This only intensified the feelings against Cauble and his workers, which soon escalated into more violence.

On Saturday evening, March 1, 1924, Cauble was behind the counter of his store in Elco, where he could usually be found on this busiest day of the week. His wife, Mary, was alone in their house when someone threw a lit stick of dynamite attached to a bomb into the yard of the home.[42] The dynamite landed near the corner of the house, but luckily an unidentified neighbor saw the sputtering fuse of the dynamite and stamped it out before it detonated. Mrs. Cauble was sitting in the house near where the bomb would have exploded.

The *Cairo Evening Citizen* took a firm stand against such violent acts of terrorism just as the *Jonesboro Gazette* had done in support of the DuBois brothers. The *Citizen* stated that county officials were united in declaring that these attempts at terrorism must stop at once. "Every county official, the sheriff and his deputies, the state's attorney, all backed by the county board to the limit are making every possible effort to bring the guilty persons to justice," stated the newspaper. It was one thing to dynamite and burn the house occupied by African American workers in Alexander County, but now they had crossed the line by endangering a White woman whose life mattered more to most of the White citizenry than did the Black farm laborers.

Three days after the assault on the Cauble home and almost two months after the attack on the Black tenant farmers, the Alexander County Board of Commissioners offered a $300 reward "for the arrest and conviction of the person or persons guilty of the recent attempts to burn, dynamite, and shoot up the buildings on the farm of Israel Cauble, near Gravel Pit Switch, north of Tamms, Illinois, and to shoot or injure the tenants on said farm."[43] The reward was the equivalent of about $5,000 a century later and would only be paid if there was a conviction (which most people knew was unlikely).

Conditions became so serious that Major William P. Greaney, commander of Company K of the Illinois National Guard at Cairo, was ordered by Adjutant General Carlos Black to go to Elco and investigate.[44] The purpose seemed to be to send a message to the band of outlaws in northeastern Alexander County that the state militia was available to be used if the situation worsened beyond the control of the sheriff. Major Greaney went to Elco, but as other investigators discovered, the people had little to say about events on the Cauble farm. Loyalty to family and neighbors outweighed any desire some of them may have had to tell what they knew about the incidents. The sheriff and his deputies were met with tight lips from residents of Elco, who would say nothing to reveal the names of the small group of White men who had resorted to terrorist tactics to drive the Black workers from the neighborhood. A large number of the citizens were in sympathy with the night riders and would not cooperate with the sheriff, and not even the $300 reward seemed able to shake loose information regarding the identities of the men.

A grand jury was called on March 12, 1924, in a special session at the county courthouse in Cairo to investigate the racial disorder in Elco. The witnesses brought in from Elco were questioned for two hours by State's Attorney Leslie Wilbourn, but they would not give enough definite information to indict anyone or issue arrest warrants.[45] City Judge Louis Marion Bradley filled the position on the bench, as Judge William N. Butler was attending a Republican convention in Harrisburg. Many more witnesses were called the second day, and now that they were required to testify under oath, some of them were more forthcoming with information.

Israel Cauble, Major Greaney, and County Commissioner William J. Johnston testified before the grand jury on Thursday morning, which led to four indictments.[46] The testimony of Johnston, who was also president of a wholesale hardware company in Cairo, suggests that perhaps someone had come forward with information in order to try to collect the reward. The Black men who were threatened and attacked at the tenant house answered questions before the jury in the afternoon. Nearly 40 witnesses, mostly Elco area farmers, were called before the grand jury adjourned late Friday afternoon.[47] Pinkerton detectives were reported to be a part of the investigation, although it is not clear who hired them.[48]

Eleven indictments were returned by the jury, and Judge Butler issued bench warrants on March 17, 1924, for the men's arrests on the charges of assault with intent to murder and destruction of property by explosives.[49]

Included were two deputy sheriffs, brothers who had recently been active in the campaign against bootleggers in the Elco area.[50] They surrendered themselves and their commissions as deputies.[51] Others were involved for whom no indictments were made, and it was reported that at least three individuals had fled from the area.[52] Once arrested, the men were brought to the county jail, located in the basement of the Cairo courthouse. The families of most of the men were able to scrape together enough money to post the $1,000 bond so the men could return home.

An examination of the 11 men and boys who were accused of leaving their homes and farms around Elco with their guns and dynamite to threaten, intimidate, and perhaps kill any Black men who believed they had a right to live in a tenant house in their neighborhood reveals nothing unusual. They were White citizens of rural Alexander County, not unlike the thousands of others living on farms in the county. Their average age was 30, and they were all natives of Illinois, most of them born in Alexander County. Four of the youngest were single, but the others were married men with children. It is not known if any of them were members of the Ku Klux Klan, which was just beginning to organize in the area, but if the charges against them were true they certainly would have been in agreement with the racist rhetoric the Klan was spewing in the 1920s.

Burley Oscar Brown was 40 years old. He was a native of rural Jonesboro in Union County and was married to Sarah Ellen White after he secured a divorce from his first wife, Mattie Jewell Sackett, in 1904. Sarah's brother, Alfred White, was married to Bessie Cauble, the only daughter of Israel Cauble. Burley was the father of two children, ages seven and nine, in 1924. He was a farmer and deputy sheriff in rural Elco and was charged with assault with intent to murder.

James Marshall Hurston was 40 and a native of Elco, where he was a farmer. He and Mary "Mollie" Smith had been married 20 years in 1924. They had five children at the time of his arrest, ranging in ages from 10 to 19. In addition to shooting with intent to kill, Hurston was charged with destruction of property by dynamiting, and his bond was set at $2,000, which he posted with William W. White, Burley Brown, and Archibald Miller as his securities.[53]

Lark Jackson Betts was 39 and a farmer in Elco, with a fifth-grade education. His first wife, Mary Jane Dillman, died in 1920, and he had been married to Mary Lillian Schilling for three years in 1924. He had five children at the time of the Elco Trouble, ranging in age from 1 to 10. He was charged with assault with intent to murder. He made his $1,000 bond with his wife's parents, Charles F. and Mary (McRaven) Schilling, as securities.[54]

Albert "Boots" Stevenson was 38 and a native of rural Delta in Alexander County. He worked hewing railroad ties and as a farm laborer. His wife of 18 years in 1924 was Mary L. Bright, and their children were 2 to 16 years old. He was charged with assault with intent to murder.

Roy Short was 31, an Elco farmer with a third-grade education. His wife was Sarah I. (Akers) Thompson, to whom he had been married for two years. They had a one-year-old daughter at the time of his arrest. Roy Short was the last to make bond and was kept in jail at Cairo for several days.[55] An ideal prisoner, he threatened to "whip" Jesse Ross (who was in jail on a charge of larceny) if he didn't stop trying to dig his way out.[56] Short made his bond on March 20, 1924, with William E. Newell as security.[57] He was charged with assault with intent to murder.

John P. Brown was 30 years old and a brother of Burley Oscar Brown. He had an eighth-grade education and was a farmer living on Diswood Road and also a deputy sheriff. John had been married seven years to Ethel Hammonds, and they had one child, a five-year-old daughter. After his marriage, John and his family lived with his parents, John Jasper and Elizabeth "Lizzie" (Baker) Brown. At the time of the Elco Trouble, his wife was pregnant with a second child, who was born a few weeks later. Deputy Brown was charged with assault with intent to murder.

Charles Clarence Raby was 29 and a farmer in rural Elco. He had a fourth-grade education. He had been married 10 years to Rana Ruth Walters. Their children in 1924 were ages six, seven, and eight. In addition to shooting with intent to kill, Raby was charged with destruction of property by dynamiting, and his bond was set at $2,000. He posted the bond on March 19, 1924, with Scott Mitchell and Jerton Harvel as securities.

George Oliver Staggs was 24, a native of Alexander County, and single. He was a laborer, probably at the silica mill, of which he would later become superintendent at Tamms. George had an eighth-grade education. Staggs left Elco and fled to Granite City, where he was arrested by St. Clair County authorities and brought to jail in Cairo the night of March 20, 1924. He was charged with assault with intent to murder.

Clyde Cecil Staggs, single, was 21 years old, a native of rural Jonesboro, and had a fourth-grade education. He was a brother of George O. Staggs. Clyde

Staggs fled Elco and was arrested with his brother at Granite City, Illinois. He was charged with assault with intent to murder.

Paul "Poodle" Dailey was 16 and a native of rural Elco. He had a third-grade education and worked on the farm of his parents, William and Isabella (Rendleman) Dailey. Charged with destruction of property by explosives, he posted bond with his father as security.[58]

Clyde Everett Tatum was 15 years old and lived with his widowed mother, Mahulda Carolina "Hulda" (Hazlewood) Raby Tatum, and his sister, Susa E. Tatum, on a farm in rural Elco. His father, William C. Tatum, died when Clyde was about 12 years old. Clyde was a half-brother of Charles Clarence Raby and like him was charged with destruction of property by explosives. Tatum was the last to be apprehended by Sheriff Roche.[59] His mother told the sheriff he was out hunting when he arrived to arrest him, but Tatum supposedly fled the county while the grand jury was in session and before indictments were returned.[60] He had not turned himself in to the sheriff at Cairo as of March 22, 1924.[61] He was later arrested and posted bond on May 13, 1924, with fellow accused Burley Brown and Charles Raby as his securities.[62]

With all the men out on bond, the May term of circuit court was set as a date for the trial to begin. All 11 men were represented by the same lawyer, David Burton Reid of Cairo, who immediately filed a motion to dismiss the charges against the Elco men on a technicality, as most of them had been grand jury witnesses; Reid's argument was that a defendant cannot testify against himself before a grand jury.[63] Judge Butler denied the motion, stating that the men were not defendants when they testified before the jury and did not become defendants until after they were indicted.[64]

While the defendants were out on bail and awaiting trial, Ku Klux Klan organizers went to Elco to recruit members and stir unrest, but it is not clear how successful the Klan was. They certainly would have found many who agreed with their message of White supremacy even if they were too poor to officially join. The incident at the Cauble tenant house in January showed that racism existed even without official Klan organization, just as it had thrived for generations before the coming of the Second Klan.

The defendants, even if they were guilty, were likely not worried about their trial. Conviction required 12 men to be in unanimous agreement about their guilt, and the accused would have felt assured that at least one man on the jury would not accept the testimony of a Black man against a White man. In fact, their case would not even come to trial. Each time trials were scheduled, there were motions to continue until the next term, a common delay tactic. This legal strategy was used continuously by the attorneys until January 1925, when charges were dismissed by State's Attorney Wilbourn because of what he called "insufficient evidence to convict any of the defendants."[65]

The prosecution's most important witness was Dan Smothers. He had identified Deputy John Brown as one of the men who had visited the house where he was staying when he was shot a year earlier, but Smothers was forced to admit that he had never seen Brown before that night, that it was dark outside, and that he was never close enough to any of the men to see them clearly. John Brown and his brother Burleigh both asserted their innocence and stated they were accused because they had offended bootleggers by enforcing Prohibition laws and that the whiskey makers were now trying to get revenge by coaching Smothers to testify against them.[66] There may have been truth in their plea, as they both likely knew that the sheriff's son, Leslie B. Roche, was selling protection to bootleggers in the county.[67]

In the end, charges were dropped and the 11 defendants went free without having to face a jury. The guilty parties who had dynamited two houses, wounded a man, and burned at least one other house were never punished by the law. They had accomplished their goal of not allowing African Americans to live north of the gravel pit switch. The 1930 census showed no Americans of African descent living in Elco Precinct. What remained was a legacy of unchecked White supremacy and a shameful, violent past.[68]

CHAPTER SEVEN

For Twenty-Six Pennies

J AMES C. WILSON HAD ALREADY closed his store two and a half miles east of Villa Ridge for the night and was in his home 50 yards away. Several neighbors who had been sitting on the front porch of the store had left for the evening and meandered back to their homes.[1] It was dark and about 10:30 Monday evening, July 21, 1924, when he heard a call from the road.[2] "Hey, Cap, open up the store, we wants to buy some groceries. We just got to have some groceries tonight." "Cap," short for captain, was a title of respect often used by Black men when talking to White men in authority during the Jim Crow era. The young man, about 19, was a stranger to Wilson but had been there earlier in the afternoon and bought a pack of cigarettes, saying he would return in the evening to buy more groceries.

He and a buddy had been loitering around the store and sitting under a tree near the Wilson home most of that day. They had flirted with Mrs. Oma Currie and her daughter, Ruby, who lived nearby, but the women had rejected their advances and returned them with insults. The Curries were not interested in the flirtatious strangers but had gotten a close look at the men during their conversation. The men had not come to Villa Ridge to accost women but rather to work in the nearby orchards picking fruit.[3] Villa Ridge was known for its orchards and fruit-producing fields, in particular strawberries, which attracted seasonal migrant pickers to the town each spring.

The two men's plans changed after one of them returned from the store where he had purchased his cigarettes. His buddy was sitting under a tree still trying to talk with the Curries when he walked back. He said privately to the other man, "Hell, I'm not going to pick any peaches. That man's got a box of money. It would be easier to get it than to pick peaches."[4] The two waited for it to get dark and for Wilson to finish his day's business.

Wilson lived in the house with his wife, Mary (Deimund) Wilson, and three daughters, Helen M., 23; Yula Amelia, 20; and Daisy May, 18.[5] The family had only lived in Villa Ridge a few years and had moved there from New Wells, a small community near Cape Girardeau, Missouri. The Wilsons had many relatives in Missouri, and, in fact, Daisy Wilson had planned to go to Cape Girardeau that day but had changed her mind so she could pick apples in the family's small orchard.

Wilson did not want to reopen the store, but the man was persistent and called out again. Grumbling about the men waiting until after he had closed the store for the night to ask for groceries, Wilson got the keys to the back door of the store and a lamp, and let the men in the front entrance. The man who had hailed him from the road did all of the talking, asking for a sack of flour and bacon. As Wilson was cutting the bacon, the other man, a couple of years older than the one who did all the talking, came from behind, put a .38 caliber Smith & Wesson in Wilson's side and said, "Stick 'em up."

Daisy Wilson had followed her father to the store to see if she could be of help with the customers and walked in as he was struggling with one of the men for the gun. She joined in the fight to help her father and picked up a scale weight and hit the man on the head.[6] The three of them fell out the back door into the darkness, and Daisy fell to the ground about 10 feet away under a cherry tree. As she got up, the man with whom her father had struggled started to run but then turned around and fired a shot, "just to be shootin'," he would later recall. Daisy Wilson fell dead, hit in the head below the left eye.

The other robber, "slightly mulatto and three inches taller than his companion," ran back into the store to steal what money he could find, a cigar box containing a pouch with 26 pennies.[7] The money that had tempted him into robbery earlier in the day must have been taken home with Wilson when he closed his store. Nothing had gone as the thieves had expected, and the two men fled the store, meeting each other in the peach orchard across the road.

Daisy's mother, hearing the commotion from the store, came out of the house with an unloaded shotgun. She stepped outside in time to hear the shot and see her daughter fall. Dropping the gun, she ran to Daisy's side. Mr. Wilson ran to retrieve shotgun shells, load the gun, and shoot across the peach orchard as the men fled into the darkness.

The two thieves ran for their lives down Meridian Road and turned at Joe Bour's place. Stopping for a moment to catch their breath and forge a plan, they decided to separate. One headed south in the direction of Mound City, about three and a half miles away, and the other, the young man who shot Daisy Wilson, variously described as "slightly mulatto" and "the yellow negro," continued on the run toward Mounds, which was to the west but closer.

Within 30 minutes of the shooting, the whole countryside around Villa Ridge was aroused by the alarm that two "colored men" (no doubt some said "n———s") had killed Miss Daisy Wilson, and so began the hunt for the men. The two Black men had not only committed murder, but they had dared to commit violence against a White woman, and the punishment for that crime, the White community believed, must be especially severe.

Hundreds of armed White men and boys, mostly farmers from the neighborhood but also men from Villa Ridge, Mounds, Mound City, Cairo, and other local towns, carrying lanterns and flashlights, searched the countryside within a five-mile radius of the store in search of the assailants.[8] There is no evidence that any Americans of African descent joined the search party. Some of the farmers from the Villa Ridge area were new members of the Ku Klux Klan, which had started recruiting a year earlier, but this was not a time to wear their robes or exchange secret handshakes and signs. They blocked and guarded the roads leading from the scene of the crime, not realizing that the two fugitives had already fled beyond the perimeter of their blockade.

Two Black men were spotted by members of the vigilante party walking near the woods by the Illinois Central Railroad tracks outside Villa Ridge. When they were ordered to stop, they became scared and broke into a run. Shots were fired at them in the dark, but they were never found. Some members of this unofficial posse thought one of the men was hit and fell but got up and kept running. The band of citizens had the same men trapped in a wooded area and began to close in on them. What was not known at the time was that the men being sought were not along the railroad near Villa Ridge, and the trigger-happy posse had shot at two innocent men, perhaps even wounding one. Their dilemma was caused by the fact that they matched the description of the two men at Wilson's store; that is, they were two young Black men. Their identities were never revealed.

Bloodhounds from Water Valley, in Graves County, Kentucky, about 50 miles away, and from Mounds, five miles away, were brought in and placed on the trail from the spot under the tree where the men had sat on the evening of the crime. Dogs from Jonesboro, Illinois, and Charleston, Missouri, were also sent for but were not used. The dogs followed the trail down Meridian Road, beyond Joe Bour's place and across the fields to the railroad tracks north of Mounds.[9]

The search was called off when word was spread early Tuesday morning that two suspects matching the robbers' description had been arrested at Mounds and were at the city jail. This was good news for the two unidentified men trapped in the woods with the posse closing in on them. The bloodhounds were pulled off their trail at the Mounds railroad yards (sometimes called "South Mounds") and sent back to Kentucky, everyone assuming the murderers had been captured. Illinois Central Special Agents Dallas Winchester and Charles H. Cruse and the Pulaski County deputies were called off from the search as well to protect the two men just arrested.

The two men in custody gave their names and addresses as Arthur Jones of 1428 Trigg Street, and Ike Brown, 21, of 1316 Helems Street, both of Memphis, Tennessee. They were arrested in the railroad yards south of Mounds near the ice plant of Central Illinois Public Services Company by Joseph Henry Bour, a 28-year-old "railroad man," and Forrest H. Moreland, the local Ku Klux Klan organizer. Moreland early on expressed doubts as to whether the two were the same men who had robbed the store and killed Daisy Wilson. The jailed men claimed they were not even in Illinois when the crime occurred.

Arthur Jones and Ike Brown were taken to the city jail in Mounds, and J. C. Wilson was brought there to view them. Wilson was still in shock after the killing of his daughter, his assault, and the armed robbery but said after a "long study" that the prisoners resembled the men who had robbed his store and killed his daughter, but he could not swear that they were the same men. Pulaski County Sheriff Ira Hudson took charge of the prisoners and decided to take them to the Wilson store so a sister of Daisy Wilson could try to identify them as the two men who had been loitering near the store the day of the robbery and murder. The trip also proved futile, when like her father, the sister said she could not make a positive identification. J. C. Wilson examined the prisoners two more times and became convinced "under mob pressure" that one of them was the man who had killed his daughter, but he still refused to swear they were the ones.[10]

Several farmers from the neighborhood who had seen the two men loitering around the store were also brought in and examined the prisoners, but no one could positively identify them as the same men, only that they were dressed the same as the men they had seen about the store. The accused men were nervous, and the crowd of hundreds of curious spectators who gathered in the yard at the Wilson home was becoming agitated and impatient. Now the accused men and their protectors began to realize that they were trapped, and Sheriff Hudson was beginning to wonder how he could get the prisoners in his charge safely to the county jail in Mound City, about seven miles away.

Seymour Welch, a 40-year-old neighbor, was among the crowd on that sweltering summer day and was overcome. A watchman at the veneer factory in Mound City, he suffered from heart trouble and is said to have muttered after viewing the bloody dead body of Daisy Wilson, "Oh, my God, the sight of that beautiful dead girl has killed me."[11] A friend, Ed B. Gore, helped Welch sit down under a tree on the lawn, but in a few minutes he was dead. His body was covered with a sheet and placed near Daisy Wilson to await the arrival of County Coroner Otis T. Hudson, the sheriff's brother. The death of Welch increased the agitation of the spectators and made the men in the crowd angrier. Now the suspects were not only accused of the murder of Daisy Wilson but of contributing to the death of Seymour Welch, a White man with a widow and six children. The crowd slowly but assuredly turned into a lynch mob, sure of the suspects' guilt and intent on providing their version of quick justice.

CHAPTER EIGHT

The Lynch Mob and the Klansman's Prayer

S HERIFF IRA HUDSON REALIZED soon after arriving at the Wilson home with his two suspects that he had made a mistake in bringing them there from the protection of their cells at the city jail in Mounds. A crowd was gathering around the house, and their number grew and became more hostile after Hudson arrived with the men. When he left in a car with the two suspects, they were pursued by several hundred men in vehicles across the hills and bottom land of Pulaski County for two hours. A direct route along Meridian Road from Villa Ridge to Mound City would have only taken a few minutes, but Sheriff Hudson was driving in circles and taking back-roads, stopping, hiding, trying to lose the pursuing mob and avoid being trapped. The mob and many others believed the men were guilty and, in fact, the front-page headline of the *Carbondale Daily Free Press* on July 22 read, "Mob Bent on Lynching, Chase Murderers of White Girl for Miles."[1] The two men were presented as "murderers" and not murder suspects, and the myth of innocent until proven guilty was not even given mention.

Despite claims to justify lynching by blaming it on an inefficient judicial system, celebrating it as frontier justice, or viewing it as an exhibition of pure democracy, lynching is murder. Lynch mobs were almost all composed of four parts, each working together to bring about the same end: to murder some-one as punishment for an alleged crime, usually before a trial was held.[2] At the heart of the mob were the leaders, the men who took charge and barked orders to the others. The men who carried the ropes, placed the noose around the victim's neck, waved and shot their guns, and did all the work involved in the execution were the leaders. Also essential were the "cheerlead-ers," the men and often women who surrounded the mob leaders and shouted encouragement to them while ridiculing and spitting on the man or woman about to be lynched. Surrounding the cheerleaders were the onlookers, usually comprising the majority of the lynch mob, who were drawn to the scene out of a morbid curiosity or a desire to witness a historic event. Also essential to a lynching were the silent citizens who knew what was happening but stayed home. They had no desire to be present but refused to speak out and condemn the actions of the mob or try to intervene to stop them. Sometimes, if one prominent member appeared and spoke out against the lynching, it could be stopped, but that was rare. The leaders in a community who hid behind drawn curtains or remained silent in the shadows, feigning ignorance about the lynching the next day, are what allowed mobs to form.

Another aspect most often underlying lynching was racism. Lynch mobs usually punished Black men, although White men committed crimes just as atrocious. Some believed that Black offenders did not deserve a fair trial. Of the more than 4,700 Americans lynched between the 1880s and World War II, 73 percent were Black.[3] Racial-terror lynching was also intended to send a message to all Americans of African descent of intimidation, forced submission, and White supremacy.

This July 1924 lynch mob posed a double threat to Sheriff Hudson—to his prisoners and to his elected position as sheriff. A 1905 Illinois antilynching law stated that if an accused person is taken from the custody of the sheriff and lynched, the governor must remove the sheriff from office. An investigation and hearing should then follow, and if the sheriff could prove he had done all in his power to protect his prisoners, then he might be reinstated. This law was used in 1909 to remove Alexander County Sheriff Frank E. Davis from office after the lynching in Cairo of Will "Froggie" James and Henry A. Salzner. Sheriff Hudson may have been concerned about losing his position if the prisoners were taken from him and lynched, but he also wanted to uphold his sworn duty to protect them.

Lynching was not merely a southern phenomenon or something that only happened in the Wild West; it happened in southern Illinois. It occurred in nearly every county in the region, not to mention more frequently in southeast Missouri and western Kentucky. There were 1,739 documented lynchings in the United States between 1900 and 1924.[4] All but 171 of them were Americans of African descent. More than a dozen lynchings or attempted lynchings occurred in Alexander and Pulaski Counties from 1900 to 1924.[5] All but one of the victims were African Americans.

A review of the most sensational of these will demonstrate the challenge that faced Sheriff Hudson. William Johnson, a 17-year-old American of

African descent, was lynched by hanging from an oak tree and his body riddled with bullets by a mob at Thebes in Alexander County on April 26,
1903.[6] He had approached a 10-year-old White girl in the barnyard of her
father, Branson Davis, near Santa Fe (renamed Fayville in 1906), and made
her scream. Napoleon Hickson, the man who was accused of putting the
rope around Johnson's neck, was tried for murder, but the outcome was a
hung jury and he was discharged.[7] Harry LaCelle was convicted of participating in the lynching, fined one hundred dollars, and sentenced to six months
in jail.[8] Several other alleged members of the lynch mob (Henry Pettit, Ed
Laish, Henry Metcalf, Henry Dixon, Fred Kenner, James Rains, C. C. Bailey, James Buster, Bryant Davis, and Lt. John F. Parker) were indicted but
were released because of insufficient evidence to convict.[9]

In another incident, Samuel A. Mason, a 40-year-old Black man, was accused of raping an 11-year-old White girl at Future City on June 10, 1904, but
many believed the girl's mother had made her accuse him of the crime and
that he was innocent. He denied the charges, and to protect him from a lynch
mob, a group of about 30 African American men armed themselves and
stood guard outside the courthouse in Cairo.[10] There was no lynching, but
several of the men protecting Mason were arrested for carrying concealed
weapons, and three Winchester rifles were found in the area around the
courthouse.[11] Mason was found guilty and sentenced to 20 years in the penitentiary at Chester. John Bingham, the sole African American on the jury,
voted for acquittal, but each of the White jurors took turns arguing with
him to get him to change his mind, and after two days he relented and voted
for conviction.[12]

Eight months later, Bob Bell, of Cairo, described as "very black, half-witted
and exceedingly ignorant," was accused of assaulting Fannie Sammons, a
16-year-old White girl, near Willard in Alexander County on February 23,
1905, and was found sleeping in a hayloft by two constables.[13] About 50 in-
furiated farmers from the neighborhood planned to lynch Bell, but the
constables took a detour through a field, and they evaded capture on their
way to take their prisoner to Cairo.[14]

Seven months later, on September 16, 1905, a quarrel between two men over
three dollars escalated, after which one of them, George Martin, fired his shotgun recklessly into a crowd while trying to hit the other man, Tom Mitchell.
He missed but hit four Black men and W. O. Bruce, an 18-year-old White
man, who died the next day. Martin was arrested and barely made it to the

Cairo city jail through a mob of White men who screamed, "Lynch the Negro! He has killed a white man!"[15]

Another mob was formed in Mounds about a year later, on July 30, 1906, to lynch 19-year-old Samuel Lee "Sam" McDonald of Perks.[16] Two days earlier, at a "negro picnic" five miles north of Ullin, Homer Harris, the operator of a merry-go-round, had forced Homer Travis, a 19-year-old man, off the ride for refusing to pay his nickel.[17] Witnesses stated McDonald gave Travis a .38 caliber pistol and told him, "Let him have it." Harris was shot and later died from his wounds. The two men fled in a "pitched gun battle," but McDonald was apprehended in Perks and taken to Ullin, where he was placed on the Illinois Central for Mounds. A mob of White men formed at Ullin and went to Mounds, where their numbers grew as they began wandering the streets of the town looking for the prisoner. The arresting deputy took McDonald to McNulty's Livery in Mounds and after dark hired a wagon and hid McDonald in the bottom. As the deputies drove the wagon toward Mound City, they were discovered and at least one shot was fired at them, but they made it safely to the county jail in Mound City, averting another lynching.[18]

The most infamous lynching was that of the aforementioned Will "Froggie" James, who was accused of the rape and murder of a White woman named Anna Pelley. He was lynched in downtown Cairo on November 11, 1909, while a crowd of thousands of spectators watched. His body was then dragged behind an automobile to the site of Pelley's murder, where it was decapitated, mutilated, and set on fire.[19] On the same night, Henry A. Salzner, a White man accused of brutally murdering his wife in front of his two infant children, was taken from the jail at Cairo and lynched.[20] A lynch mob also formed outside the jail in Cairo, which held Arthur Alexander, another suspect in the Pelley rape and murder. As Alexander was being removed from the city on November 13, 1909, he was protected by Illinois National Guardsmen. One gray-haired woman stepped from the crowd and yelled, "Men, will you be cowards? Will you see the black demon escape? Will you see your daughters murdered by a black fiend? I call on you to take this negro murderer and give him the fate he deserves." The soldiers stepped forward, pointing their bayonets at the crowd, and another lynching was avoided.[21]

Soon after, on February 18, 1910, John Pratt, a Black man accused of purse snatching in Cairo, and his alleged accomplice, Lincoln Wilson of Grand Chain, were saved from lynching by a dozen African American deputies who fired into the mob that had surrounded the courthouse, killing Alexander

Halliday, a member of a prominent White family in Cairo.[22] In September 1913, two Black men, Walter Johnson and an unnamed man, went from Cairo to Tamms and allegedly tried to pass a one-dollar bill, which they were accused of having "raised" to five dollars. The store clerk refused to accept the bill, and they allegedly fired shots at him as they fled the store.[23] A mob pursued and when bloodhounds were brought from Anna about midnight, Johnson was found dead, shot in the back in a field about a mile south of Tamms.[24]

Another attempt at lynching occurred on June 17, 1919, in Pulaski County. Caylour Wisdom, a 32-year-old Black man, was hunted down by a lynch mob after he slashed his wife's throat near Olmsted.[25] He fled toward Ullin but was pursued by a mob of men from Grand Chain and Olmsted who took him to woods where he was abused, shot in the back, and left for dead. He was later found barely alive by a constable and taken to jail in Mound City. Wisdom recovered and pled guilty with the understanding that he would not get the death penalty. He was tried, and although the state's attorney stated he was "simple minded," he was sentenced to life in prison at hard labor on July 30, 1919.[26] These and other related incidents were a part of the county's recent past in 1924. Sheriff Hudson was not being overly cautious; he had legitimate reasons to be concerned.

Sheriff Hudson and his prisoners, not thinking they could make it to the jail in Mound City, stopped at the jail at City Hall in Mounds, where they were locked inside. A mob of about six hundred began to gather around the City Hall "bent on lynching," and automobiles arrived with more men until numbers increased to about one thousand.[27] Some were curious spectators from the town, while others were inciting the leaders of the mob to storm the jail and lynch the men inside. Sheriff Hudson, who had as many as 12 deputies to back him up, addressed the crowd and made what one newspaper called a "strong impression," but the mob did not disperse.[28] Many in the crowd were likely Klansmen, as recruitment was at its peak in Pulaski County. However, robed Klansmen never participated in lynchings in the 1920s, partly because lynchers did not need to hide their identity and had little fear of being prosecuted.[29]

Forest Hazel Moreland, the organizer of the Ku Klux Klan in Pulaski County who had led the citizens' pursuit of Miss Wilson's murderers, stood above the crowd and asked it to pray with him. He was convinced that the two men in custody, whom he had helped arrest, were not murderers, but the challenge was to place that idea in the minds of the mob. The men removed their hats and listened to what Moreland had to say. His voice rang out above the now silent crowd as he shouted, "God forgive these people" for their attempted violence. The rest of his 10-minute prayer is not recorded, but after he said "amen," the crowd remained calm, replaced their hats, looked around for a sign from the mob leaders, and slowly began to disperse. What he said in his prayer is unknown, but his words touched a nerve with those in the audience who were likely expecting to find an ally in Moreland. The *Pulaski Enterprise* recorded that Moreland's prayer "had a magical effect in silencing the mob and quieting their emotions."[30]

There is something ironic about the organizer of the Ku Klux Klan intervening to rescue from an angry lynch mob two African American men accused of murdering a White woman. Moreland had been the one who made a citizen's arrest of the two suspects in the Mounds train yard but had immediately expressed doubts that they were the guilty parties. Another factor in discouraging the mob was Sheriff Hudson's firm statement to the crowd that he and his deputies would defend the prisoners with force if necessary. Moreland's role in quieting the violent intentions of the mob was crucial, and he knew the Klan leadership preferred that the organization not be connected with violence in the press. His actions would make great propaganda in the pro-Klan press, which painted him as a hero and promoted him as evidence that they were nonviolent.

Moreland helped recruit 16 special deputies from those assembled, likely fellow Klan members, to aid the sheriff in getting his prisoners the rest of the way to Mound City. He even volunteered to be one of the deputies to guard the prisoners at the Pulaski County jail adjacent to the courthouse in Mound City. Hudson eventually delivered his prisoners to the safety of the jail and placed them under guard by a "score" of deputies. Both Arthur Jones and Ike Brown must have breathed a deep sigh of relief as they heard the cell door close behind them at the Pulaski County jail, even though the threat of lynching had followed them to that town. A lynching was averted for the time being at Mounds by the Klansman's prayer and the sheriff's strong words, but an angry crowd of between one thousand and thirteen hundred persons was now growing outside the courthouse in Mound City, and many still were convinced of the men's guilt and wanted action.[31]

After Jones and Brown were secured in jail, the search resumed for other suspects, as there seemed to be serious doubt developing among law enforcement officers that those under custody were the murderers. The initial description that was supplied by the two Currie women from Villa Ridge was vague. The law officers were looking for two Black males about five feet, eight inches, one wearing a dark suit and the other a light shirt. Two Black men, supposedly promising suspects, were being held in Humboldt, Tennessee, after being seen in Cairo and boarding a Mobile and Ohio train in Tamms, a few miles northwest in Alexander County. Sheriff Hudson and J. C. Wilson traveled to Humboldt where Wilson said the two men were definitely not the murderers.[32] Another suspect, Fred Hale, was arrested in Cairo and brought to the Mound City jail. Suspects matching the description of the two men were also rounded up in southern Illinois, southeast Missouri, and western Kentucky. Witnesses were brought to the jail in Mound City for further questioning and to identify the suspected robbers and murderer. Those involved in the investigation also expanded to include railroad detectives and the Illinois National Guard as the entire region became more volatile.

CHAPTER NINE

Railroad Detectives and the National Guard

P
ULASKI AND ALEXANDER County law enforcement officers were not the only ones investigating the murder. The chief special agent for the St. Louis division of the Illinois Central Railroad, John Henry Miskel, lived in Carbondale, and he ordered all of his detectives to "spread the net" for the two men wanted for the murder of Daisy Wilson.[1] A "special agent" is usually a detective working for the federal or state government to investigate a crime, but Miskel was a special agent for the railroad. "Railroad policemen" were more than just security guards for the railroad and its passengers and often were involved in investigations of crimes connected to railroads. Many were trained detectives, often more qualified in that work than local law enforcement officers.

The description Miskel provided his special agents was more detailed than what had been earlier released in the newspapers. Suspect No. 1 was 20 years old, stood five feet, 10 inches tall, weighed 135 or 140 pounds, and was Black. He wore greasy blue coveralls and a jumper, a dark shirt, and a blue cap on the side of his head. Suspect No. 2 was 19 or 20 years old, five feet, six or seven inches tall, weighed 130 pounds, and was Black. He wore dark-colored trousers with the seat almost torn out, a light-colored shirt, and a gray cap.[2]

After Special Agent Charles O. McKinney investigated a rumor that a Black man carrying a gun was seen two miles north of Mounds on Wednesday morning, he commandeered a speedster automobile and headed north. Alexander County Sheriff James Stephen Roche and his deputy son, Leslie Roche, heard the same rumor and also went to investigate. The suspect was located, but he was not carrying a gun and was not held for further questioning. All young Black men living in Alexander and Pulaski Counties who resembled the description must have been nervous about being suspected, arrested, or worse.

Evidence confirming the innocence of Jones and Brown continued to grow. Special Agent McKinney identified them as the same men he had seen ride into Mounds on a freight train headed north after the time of the murder. A railroad brakeman at Mounds came forward with an alibi for the two men, willing to swear they were on a freight train he had brought into Mounds early Tuesday morning about 1 A.M. A White boy confirmed the brakeman's testimony and said he had hitched a ride on the freight with the two men at Memphis, Tennessee, and rode it into Mounds with them. The two Currie women also swore positively that the two men under arrest were not the same men outside the Wilson store the day Daisy Wilson was shot.

But the lynch mob in front of the jail in Mound City, even when confronted with the truth, refused to admit that Jones and Brown might be innocent. Hundreds of "drunken and mad men" stood vigil outside the courthouse. The *Pulaski Enterprise* reported that "the courthouse square and streets adjoining were one tangle of automobiles and excited humanity. Many cars were parked bearing Herrin and Marion name plates," but most of the people in the crowd were from Pulaski and neighboring Alexander Counties.[3] Local newspapers tried to convince their readers that the leaders of the lynch mob were "outside agitators" from out of state or other counties. The *Cairo Evening Citizen* clearly stated that none of the farmers from the area around Villa Ridge were in the mob, and that sentiment was echoed by the Pulaski County newspaper.[4]

A climax was reached when some of the men swarmed close to the deputies standing guard. Fearing the worst, Sheriff Hudson smuggled his three prisoners—the two men arrested in Mounds, Jones and Brown, and the one apprehended in Cairo, Fred Hale, out of the jail early Tuesday evening to a secret location for safekeeping. Hudson sent Deputy Albert J. Riding to get a curtained touring car about 7 P.M. and drive it back to the jail. The three prisoners were taken out the kitchen door, placed in the back seat, and a quilt was thrown over them. Riding and James Wilson, a 44-year-old African American Pulaski County deputy armed with a sawed-off shotgun, drove the three men in Riding's car. Hudson and Special Agent Winchester intercepted the car downtown and got in.[5] The prisoners were then driven about 55 miles to Murphysboro, said to have the most secure jail in southern Illinois, but on arrival, Jackson County Sheriff Crillon Edgar White advised them that another mob was forming in Murphysboro and that Hudson should take his men to Chester, the location of the Southern Illinois Penitentiary, about 30 miles away, where they arrived safely about 1 A.M.[6]

Deputy Sheriff Charles Walbridge was left in charge of the other 11 prisoners in jail, all Black. Since Sheriff J. S. Roche of Alexander County had sent several deputies with "riot guns" to help defend the prisoners in the Pulaski County jail, Walbridge had about 20 deputies under his command.[7] He feared for the safety of the remaining prisoners, his fellow law officers, and members of the mob, and the deputy sent an urgent request to Governor Len Small about 1 A.M. to send the National Guard from Cairo.[8] Despite telling the mob leaders several times throughout the night that the prisoners were no longer there, the mob did not believe Deputy Walbridge.

The local press agreed that the mob comprised chiefly young men and boys, many of whom were drunk.[9] One masked young man falsely claimed he was "Reverend Anderson" of Cairo, one of the Klan recruiters, and thereby sought to counter the prayer of the Klansman, convince the mob that God was on their side, and energize them to rush the jail. This "short, stout, red-faced man," disguising the lower part of his face with a handkerchief, denounced the deputies and threatened to throw a hand grenade if the three Black men were not turned over to the mob.[10] He claimed to be from St. Louis and that he had come for the lynching. He also said he was a veteran who had served with the American Expeditionary Force in France during World War I, and this assertion seemed to be supported by the presence of four men in National Guard uniforms who were with him.[11] The Reverend W. P. Anderson had gone from Cairo to Mound City to offer his services and was sworn in as a deputy sheriff and was not a member of the mob. The young man posing as the minister was not immediately identified and later said his actions were only intended as a joke on Anderson.[12]

Hundreds of shots were fired in the air and violence seemed imminent. Profanity was thrown at the deputies along with rocks, and the mob seemed to be waiting on a leader to lead them to attack the jail.[13] Two leaders of the mob emptied their revolvers several times by firing across the courthouse lawn. At least one shot was fired through the window of the jailhouse where Sheriff Hudson lived with his wife, Retta (Gher) Hudson, and their 17-year-old son, Ira Hudson Jr. The bullet went through the living room and lodged in the kitchen wall. A bullet also went through a courthouse window and lodged in the vault in the county clerk's office.

Among the crowd was a "grey-haired, weather-beaten farmer" who harangued the mob with these words: "Just think of that pretty girl killed by those negroes. Supposing it was your daughter they killed, what would you do then? I know what I'd do. I'd lynch them. I tell you, men, cowards can stand around and talk, but it takes nerve to do something. All ready, let's go!"[14] Perhaps the mob was too young or chemically impaired to respond, and no action was taken. He then began to make strange noises, which brought several prisoners to the cell windows to peer out, as well as some of the guards, who peeked from courthouse doors and windows.

A few members of the Illinois National Guard, wearing their uniforms, drawn there out of curiosity and not in an official capacity, were among the mob when it first assembled outside the jail. They came on the interurban from Cairo after the day's drill, and one of them playfully sounded his bugle, frightening some of the crowd by making them think the National Guard had already arrived. When the guardsmen realized that the situation was more serious than they thought, they rushed back to Cairo before the tension escalated.[15]

Rocks were thrown at the deputies on guard and shots fired near them. The deputies showed restraint and did not return the fire at first despite the curses and profanity shouted at them from the crowd. They stood a patient watch on the jail from the porch and in the courthouse. The *Cairo Evening Citizen* reported, "That no one was killed or seriously injured during the disturbance which got under way at 9 o'clock and continued until 12:30 is nothing less than a miracle."[16]

Several times the mob became bolder and moved forward to storm the jail, but shots fired by those in the front scared the mob, and they retreated to safety. Some men tried to shoot out an arc lamp used as a streetlight, but they missed. As if it was a game, a boy picked up a rock and hurled it at the light, proudly breaking it with his first throw. Hiding in the darkness, individuals in the mob were further protected from being identified, which emboldened them even more. They resumed throwing rocks at the deputy guards and the courthouse windows.[17]

To prevent a storming of the jail and more mob violence, a committee composed of three of the leaders of the group was allowed to come inside and search the jail cells to see that the prisoners they wanted to lynch had been taken away. One of the number was a masked young man who had claimed to be a World War I veteran, perhaps the same man who had earlier posed as the Reverend W. P. Anderson.[18] When the inspectors of the jail made their report to the mob, shouts of "liars" and "cowards" were made.[19]

Finally, between 12:30 and 1 A.M., another group from the mob was disarmed and taken through the jail and courthouse. Apparently they were more convincing than their predecessors because after their report the mob began to fade away. By the time Company K of the 130th Infantry of the Illinois National Guard, numbering between 90 and 100, arrived from Cairo by rail about 1:30 Wednesday morning, July 23, everything had begun to quiet down in Mound City. The demonstration ended by 3 A.M., and the mob dissipated and returned to their homes.[20] When Sheriff Hudson returned Wednesday morning at 4:35, he found Company K of the Illinois National Guard in charge of the town. The National Guardsmen spent the next morning playing a game of baseball on the courthouse baseball field and went back to Cairo Wednesday afternoon but were only minutes away via the interurban train if they received orders to return.

Although one of the men under arrest as a suspect was reportedly overheard asking the other what he did with "the gun," their alibi was strong. The growing sentiment was that none of the three men who had been spirited away to safety in Murphysboro and Chester were the murderers of Daisy Wilson, but it was decided to keep them under arrest "with a possibility that they will be connected with a robbery or two."[21] Sheriff Hudson began arranging for rewards of up to $1,000 for the capture of the true criminals. He asked Governor Small for a $500 reward from the state and hoped a similar amount could be raised locally. No one was forthcoming with pledges of money, and he posted a notice of a $200 reward that was published in the weekly county newspaper, the *Pulaski Enterprise*, on Friday, July 25, 1924.

One new clue came to the attention of the sheriff from Oma and Ruby Currie, the women who had been near the scene of the murder of Daisy Wilson. They told him that the larger of the two men who had tried to make a date with them told them his name was John Crowder and that he lived in Carbondale.[22] The special agents of the Illinois Central assisting in the investigation found that there was a man named John Crowder who had once lived in Carbondale and who matched the description of one of the suspects. Another Carbondale resident told Special Agents Miskell and William Wilding Underwood, of Centralia, that Crowder had returned to town the morning after the murder and that he had tried to dispose of a .38 caliber revolver, the same type of gun used to kill Daisy Wilson.[23]

The investigation also began to focus on Fred Hale *alias* Fred Bailey, 20, of 327 Twenty-Third St. in Cairo, who had been arrested as a suspect there and taken to Mound City and then to Murphysboro and Chester. Hale was viewed in his cell by James C. Wilson, who was positive that he was not the man who had killed his daughter. Wilson and other witnesses also stated clearly that Hale was not involved in the robbery or murder, and Wilson even said that he could not be certain that the same men seen loafing around the store were the same men as the murderers.[24] Hale and his companion, Hess Conner, 22, of 218 Twenty-Seventh St., had left Cairo Monday morning in search of work.[25] Witnesses claimed they saw Hale in Villa Ridge the afternoon of the murder walking from the railroad tracks in the direction of the Wilson store. Hale denied being in Villa Ridge that day, and his friend, Hess Conner, could not be found, which further aroused suspicions against them.

While investigators were diligently searching for the murderers, the funeral of Daisy Wilson was held Wednesday afternoon at the Wilson home. Hundreds of citizens of Pulaski and Alexander Counties and elsewhere attended, many more than could possibly assemble in the house or even in the front yard. Flowers were heaped around the casket. The Reverend Charles Robert Dunlap, pastor of Immanuel Lutheran Church in Cairo, where Daisy Wilson had attended church when she briefly worked in Cairo, preached the funeral sermon. The body was taken from her home near Villa Ridge by train to Mounds, where an even larger crowd awaited. Burial was in Beech Grove Cemetery at Mounds.

The search was narrowing, and efforts had increased in the ongoing search for Hess Conner since the arrest of Hale, but Conner could not be found where he lived at the home of his aunt Julia Bryant, at 218 Twenty-Seventh St., Cairo.[26] The police focused on Conner after he told a woman in Cairo that he was wanted by the police and had to get out of town. She then shared the news with Henry Douglas, a Black Alexander County deputy, who told the police chief. Cairo Chief of Police James Gilmore went to the house to question Conner's aunt, and she nervously denied a man being there. A man was subsequently found in a search of the house, although it was not Conner, and this attempted deception just further raised the suspicions of the officers.

Conner, knowing the police were looking for him, had gone on the run and was hoping to hop a freight train and make his escape from Cairo but was waiting until dark. A young man stumbled onto Conner late Friday afternoon hiding in some weeds in Future City, an unincorporated town on the north side of Cairo. Conner panicked and attacked him, assuming he was an officer come to arrest him.[27] The unidentified man knocked Conner to the ground three times while trying to subdue him, but Conner picked up a brick and knocked the young man down and made his escape.

Conner ran toward the Big Four railroad tracks and was pursued by John Whitfield, an Alexander County deputy sheriff of African descent. Several shots were fired and Conner was ordered to halt. Conner was arrested under charges of disorderly conduct and assault and taken to the county jail in Cairo, where he was questioned by Deputy Sheriff Leslie Roche and Jailer Richard Fitzgerald. He denied being in Villa Ridge on Monday, claiming to have been at his sister's house in Mound City at the time of the murder. When officers questioned his sister, Mattie Lee Wade, she told them he had come to her house about midnight and scratched at the window to be let into the house. After spending the night, he left early the next morning to return to Cairo. His alibi compromised, Conner was then falsely told by officers that Hale had made a complete confession. Conner was "stunned speechless" but still continued steadfast in his denial of any involvement in the crime.

"Two Villa Ridge negroes"—Tilford Cross, a farmer, and a man named Lee—positively identified Conner and Hale as the two men they had seen in Villa Ridge on Monday before the murder. Conner was again interrogated by Illinois Central Detective John H. Miskel, Murphysboro Policeman Dave Holder, Dallas Winchester, and a Black Pulaski County deputy, James "Jim" Wilson.[28] Thinking further denials useless, Conner was ready to make a statement, and left alone in his cell with Deputy Wilson, Conner confessed shortly before noon that he killed Daisy Wilson. He had falsely given his name as John Crowder and his residence as Carbondale to the two women in front of the Wilson Store on the day of the murder.[29] Immediately after Conner made the statement of his guilt, Deputy Leslie Roche rushed him to the Pulaski County jail, where he gave a more detailed confession before State's Attorney Loren Boyd and was then quietly returned to the jail in Cairo. Informed of Conner's confession, Hale made his own on Sunday to Deputy Sheriff Dallas Winchester.

To prevent the formation of another lynch mob, Conner was taken at once to an undisclosed jail in a distant county. He was first driven to Mound City National Cemetery by Deputy Roche, transferred to another car, and then hurried north. On Tuesday, July 29, 1924, the Pulaski County grand jury indicted Conner and Hale for first-degree murder.[30]

A meeting of about a hundred men was held with representatives from every voting precinct in Pulaski County to discuss the recent events, but who organized the meeting is not clear. The men chose Milton Dee Brelsford, a farmer in America Precinct and president of the Pulaski County Farm Bureau, as their spokesman, and he requested permission to address the court, which was meeting with the grand jury at the courthouse in Mound City just as they recessed at noon on Monday.[31] Brelsford asked that Judge Dewitt T. "Dee" Hartwell, of Marion, and State's Attorney Boyd "do everything possible to give the case against the negroes the right of way. We do not believe in mob rule, but we believe speedy justice is necessary."[32]

Forest H. Moreland, the Klan organizer, spoke next and repeated the demands for a speedy trial. He also commended Pulaski County Sheriff Hudson for his work. Moreland then announced that the Klan was offering an additional $200 reward to add to that raised by the sheriff. It was grandstanding on Moreland's part to offer a reward for evidence leading to the apprehension of the killer since the sheriff already had a confessed killer and his accomplice in custody. Perhaps Moreland was hoping the reward might entice more witnesses to come forward with evidence against Conner and Hale to ensure their convictions.

Judge Hartwell calmly and respectfully listened to the citizens' words, and if offended by the lecture to have a speedy trial, he did not show it. He told the men in the courtroom that Conner and Hale would be given a fair trial and ample protection. He also warned them that he would not tolerate any disorder. "If we must call out the National Guard, we'll call it," he informed them. The threats of lynching had subsided with the assurances of speedy justice. It seemed likely that the men who were members of the lynch mob would get to witness a legal hanging rather than participate in a lynching, and they seemed content with that.

The unsung hero of the week's events was Deputy Jim Wilson. He was Sheriff Hudson's "right hand man," protecting and transporting the prisoners and "riding shotgun" side by side with the sheriff in the most dangerous situations. He was also the man who was most instrumental in securing confessions from Hess Conner and Fred Hale. Wilson knew that without implicated suspects, mobs were most likely to form, bringing greater dangers for all Americans of African descent in Pulaski County. The mob in Mound City had been judged capable of lynching *all* the Black prisoners in the Pulaski County jail on that July night.[33] Unfortunately, Deputy Wilson received little credit for his actions in the local press.[34]

Sheriff Hudson seems to have been vindicated in the press. The *Cairo Bulletin* stated that the people of Pulaski County had cause to be grateful to their sheriff because they were kept from committing a murder "no less atrocious than that which they sought to avenge and the community was saved from a disgraceful blot on its reputation" such as had been experienced by Cairo 15 years earlier following the lynchings of James and Salzner.[35] There was also praise for the law enforcement officers at the courthouse. "Stoned and reviled by the mob, they sat immovable with guns across their knees, hoping they would not be required to fire into the crazed throng. They might have been justified once or twice in wiping out the whole mob with a dozen well placed shots from the riot guns, but decent humanity and Christian charity won out."[36]

The other key figure that stymied the attempted lynchings at Mounds and Mound City was the unlikely hero Klan leader Forest H. Moreland. His prayer contributed a great deal in dispersing the mob at Mounds and averting the lynching of two innocent men. He had been instrumental in recruiting more deputies to guard the prisoners as they were taken to the jail in Mound City. It seems unlikely that he felt any guilt or even realized his part and that of the Ku Klux Klan in initially creating the lynch mob, but he had averted the murders of two innocent men.

CHAPTER TEN

The Trial of Hale and Conner

THE MOST IMPORTANT QUESTION at the trial of Fred Hale and Hess Conner was not whether the men were guilty since they had confessed to their crime. What was left to be determined was their punishment, and most citizens were anticipating a hanging. The prisoners were totally defeated, despondent, and ready to accept their fate, even if that meant death; the trial was a formality they wanted to be over as quickly as possible if it could not be avoided entirely. They did not seem to care that the rush to a speedy trial might hamper their right to a fair trial, but if they had demanded more time, a death penalty might have been avoided.

To maintain order, a request was made to Governor Small for a return of the Illinois National Guard, but the request was denied. Six regular and 76 special deputies were called in to protect the prisoners and were given blue ribbons to wear as badges. They lined the corridors of the courthouse as the prisoners were moved from the jail to the courtroom. Spectators allowed into the courthouse for the trial were first searched for guns by Deputies Charles Henry Cruse and Albert J. Riding, and the courtroom remained orderly.

Surrounded by armed deputies wielding shotguns, Fred Hale and Hess Conner were brought into the second-floor courtroom at the Mound City courthouse on Wednesday, July 30, 1924, at 10 A.M.[1] Charles Sumner "Carl" Miller and Judge William Ambrose Wall were appointed their public defenders by Judge Hartwell since the prisoners were indigent.[2] Both were prominent and experienced attorneys living in Mound City. Wall was 59 years old, a native of Anna in Union County, and a Pulaski County judge. Miller was 45 years old, a native of Villa Ridge, and had previously served as Pulaski County state's attorney. Hale and Conner were advised not to plead guilty, but they adamantly insisted on testifying and making their confessions in court. The men also waived their right to a jury trial, again ignoring the guidance of their legal counsel, perhaps thinking it would be a less painful ordeal to be judged by one man than 12. Four times the judge asked them if they understood the consequences of their guilty pleas, and each time they answered yes. Their attorneys told the judge that they had no right to insist that their clients submit the case to a jury, and, in fact, the defendants emphatically told them that they did not even want a trial. They just wanted to be sentenced and to get the ordeal over as quickly as possible.[3]

The trial before the judge began the day after they were indicted and just two hours after their attorneys were appointed. The first witness in the trial, James C. Wilson, was called as soon as the defendants had a short meeting with their lawyers. Wilson recounted the night of his daughter's murder, and the lead bullet that had killed her was presented as evidence. The law enforcement officers who first heard the confessions of the two men testified, and then their signed confessions were read to the court. Oma and Ruby Currie also testified that Hale and Conner were the same men who had been loitering around the Wilson store the day of the murder. Importantly, Oma had earlier picked the men out of a lineup of 22 men held in the county jail.

When Hale was called to the witness stand and rose to testify, a bench seating spectators in the rear of the courtroom collapsed under the weight; it sounded like a gunshot when it collapsed, and the people seated there crashed to the floor. As the courtroom began to settle down and after recovering from the scare, Hale took his seat on the witness stand. He corroborated the testimonies of other witnesses and offered no defense for his actions. Conner also was called to testify and said the other witnesses had told the truth of what had happened. He concluded his testimony by saying, "I pleads guilty and begs the honor of the court."

The trial was over quickly and ended Wednesday night about 9:45, the same day it started, with the judge sentencing Hess Conner to hang on Friday, October 17, the earliest date the law allowed. The date was chosen by the judge because it was at least 10 days after the next meeting of the Illinois Supreme Court, which made it the soonest time at which the execution could legally be scheduled.[4] The rush to execution was intended to stop the possibility of another attempt at lynching and pacify those in the public who demanded a speedy and satisfactory conclusion of the trial. Conner did not move or show any emotion whatsoever when the judge pronounced his sentence. "He has taken everything with stoical indifference," according to the

Mound City newspaper account.[5] The circuit court record stated that Conner "stood mute and said nothing."[6]

Fred Hale sank into his chair terrified when Conner's verdict was given but straightened and was relieved to get a lesser sentence since he had not carried a gun.[7] He was sentenced to hard labor on the rock pile in the Southern Illinois Penitentiary at Chester "for the remainder of his entire and natural life."[8] As was typical in life sentences for violent crimes, on each anniversary of the killing, he was to be put in solitary confinement to reflect on what he had done. Pointing his finger at Conner, Judge Hartwell said, "I cannot ignore the fact that a big strong man like you shot to death a beautiful little girl, who, unarmed and defenseless, came heroically to the rescue of her father. Would that these who the law places here to protect you men tonight could have been at hand to protect the innocent and defenseless child."[9] When the sentence was given, the "sweltering" courtroom and hallways were packed with about eight hundred spectators, who had remained silent and respectful during the sentencing.

Judge Hartwell also remarked how fortunate it was that the lynching of the wrong men had not occurred and praised Sheriff Hudson for his work in preventing that lynching and in protecting the other two men, Hale and Conner, who were actually guilty of the murder and robbery. Then the sheriff was given the official order, which read, "Now, therefore, we do command you, that you do, on Friday, the 17th day of October, A. D. 1924, between the hours of nine o'clock in the forenoon and four o'clock in the afternoon of said day, take the body of him, the said Hess Conners [*sic*], who is now confined in the common jail of Pulaski County, and within the walls of said jail, or an enclosure adjacent and connected with said jail, and that you do then and there, hang him, the said Hess Conners [*sic*], by the neck until he is dead."[10]

After the sentencing, a narrow path was made through the crowded courthouse, and the prisoners, shackled and with heads downturned, were marched out of the courtroom. They went down the stairs and then across the courthouse lawn to their cells in the county jail, under the stares and whispers of the solemn crowd of spectators. The men were tried, convicted, and sentenced only nine days after the crime and 24 hours after their confession.

Hess Conner, called "Hessie" when he was a boy, was born March 31, 1902, in Gibson County, Tennessee, near Trenton. His father, Paul Conner, died when he was just a small child, and his mother married his stepfather, James A. Nash, when Hessie was only seven. He came from a large family and had three sisters, two brothers, one half-brother, and two half-sisters.[11] He attended school up to the eighth grade and in his early 20s moved to Cairo, where his aunt lived. He worked first as a shoeshine boy in the shops of two White barbers in Cairo, Claude Blessing and Thermon Barta Swain. Conner was working as a waiter at the prestigious Halliday Hotel in Cairo as late as June before the July murder of Daisy Wilson.

Early on Monday morning, October 13, 1924, Hess Conner heard the carpenters outside his cell constructing the stairs and rails for the scaffold (borrowed from Jackson County) from which he was sentenced to hang in four days.[12] According to the *Carbondale Daily Free Press*, Conner had presented "a bold front" until the first load of lumber arrived, and then he "visibly wilted."[13] Conner paced up and down his cell more rapidly and smoked cigarettes almost incessantly, but he maintained his stoic, matter-of-fact attitude about the situation up to the end.

Conner's girlfriend, whose name is not recorded in any known accounts, made her last visit to him in jail on Saturday before his planned execution, but he claimed he had no desire to see his wife, from whom he was separated, or their daughter. Conner was also visited by several ministers while in jail. The only hope Conner expressed was that his mother, Mrs. Lela A. Nash, would be able to "scrape together enough money to come from her home in the cotton fields of Tennessee and visit him before his death" and then give his body a burial in Tennessee, where he had grown up.[14] This all seemed unlikely.

Two days before the scheduled execution, Governor Small granted Conner a reprieve, postponing the hanging until January 16, 1925.[15] The superintendent of pardons and paroles of Illinois, Will Colvin, said that it did not make any difference to the State of Illinois if the man was executed in October or January.[16] No legal efforts for an appeal were made on behalf of Conner by his court-appointed attorneys, and the defendant did not desire one.[17] David Burton Reid, a White lawyer in Cairo, acted at the request of several Americans of African descent in that town to formally ask for a reprieve from the governor because he claimed Conner had been of "unsound mind since boyhood."[18] Reid, the same lawyer who represented the 11 men indicted in the Elco Trouble in May 1924, said, "Humanitarian reasons largely prompted me to intercede for Conner. I am opposed to capital punishment in any form."

One could argue that there were no good reasons for African Americans in Pulaski County to protest the execution of Hess Conner. He confessed his guilt and he was not from Pulaski County, although his sister lived in Mound City. Neither the pastors of the African American churches in Pulaski County, leading Black businessmen, nor prominent Black county politicians publicly condemned the lynch mob or protested the speedy trial of Conner or his quick sentencing. If anything, there was resentment against him for what he had done to trouble the waters and create even more animosity toward them from Whites in the county. As for Conner, he was initially unaware that efforts were being made to save him from the gallows and was surprised to hear of the news of his reprieve.

Fearing that the reprieve might set off renewed mob activity in Mound City, the authorities took him back to the strong jail in Murphysboro where he remained through December 1924. Conner's fate seemed to come down to his mental stability. He was taken to the state prison in Chester in early December to be examined by a committee of three physicians to report on his mental competence and sanity.[19] Drs. Albert R. Carter, Oscar Burton Ormsby, and William Henry Evans, all from Murphysboro, examined Conner and found him to be sane and eligible for execution, and he was returned to Mound City.

In early January 1925, Conner was returned to his "death cell" at the Pulaski County jail. Sheriff Hudson said he was a model prisoner and during the last week of his life was given anything he asked for to eat. "I have made my peace with God and am ready to die," Conner told Sheriff Hudson.[20] He had professed conversion to Christianity in October 1924 and received the sacrament of communion. He also said he would do his best to walk to the scaffold and "die game" to make the execution easier for Hudson, in whom he had a "child-like trust."[21] Despite his vow, a few days before his execution, Conner began to show signs of extreme anxiety and collapsed in his cell. He was so weak he could barely get off his cot and only responded to Sheriff Hudson's questions in weak monosyllables. A physician was called, and it was his opinion that Conner was actually sick and "broken down with fear."[22]

The scaffold that had been disassembled and stored away was taken out of storage in January and erected again on the courthouse lawn at Mound City by William F. Wiley, a carpenter from Mounds, and his helper, Martin Bolar, a railroad brakeman living in Mound City. A stockade around the scaffold had blown down in the fall of 1924 and had to be rebuilt. The workers also dug a pit three feet deep beneath the scaffold so that the drop of Conner's body would be about nine feet.

This was the second state execution performed in Pulaski County.[23] The first person to be publicly executed was Eli Bugg, who had been hanged by Pulaski County Sheriff James Ray Weaver nearly 20 years earlier, on Friday, February 17, 1905.[24] Bugg, a resident of Mounds, and Will Cross, of Villa Ridge, partners in a gambling booth, had attended a picnic and barbecue at Wetaug on July 23, 1904, where trouble arose between Cross and Chris Mathis, who struck Cross and knocked him down. Mathis later apologized and the two reconciled and were sharing a bottle of whisky when Bugg, who had gone in search of a revolver, returned. He told Cross, "This is a damn poor way to settle a thing like that, with a drink of whisky. If that damned 'n———' was in Mounds, he would have been dead long ago. Shoot the son of a bitch."[25] After the shot was fired, Cross and Bugg fled, and Cross was never caught. Bugg was apprehended, convicted of inciting murder, and sentenced to hang.[26] Bugg had earlier been convicted in Pulaski County in 1897 of killing a White butcher, Carl Arnold, and sentenced to prison but was pardoned by Governor Richard Yates Jr. and released in 1902.[27] The *Cairo Evening Citizen* said of Bugg on the day of his hanging, "He was a fine looking negro when dressed in a good suit and wearing a white tie."[28] About two hundred people were allowed in as witnesses, including 13 sheriffs, while a thousand others stood around on the common grounds of the courthouse outside the stockade.[29] The hanging of Conner was assured to create even more interest.

Sheriff Hudson sought the expert advice of "the traveling hangman" George Phillip "Phil" Hanna, "a wealthy bachelor politician" from Epworth, near Carmi. His services were often requested by sheriffs in southern Illinois, southern Indiana, and western Kentucky, and he made the final inspection of the gallows the day before the execution. A weight equal to that of Conner's body was dropped through the trapdoor to test the rope. Hanna had brought the rope, provided by the Saline County sheriff and which had been used in hangings five times previously, tied the hangman's noose, and even brought a backup rope in case that one broke.

Hanna was fascinated with hangings and served as the gallows inspector when such services were needed. This was the 50th execution he was to witness. Hanna saw his first hanging, that of Fred Behme in McLeansboro 28 years earlier on December 4, 1896. It was a bungled job, and Behme slowly strangled to death rather than had his neck broken. After witnessing this tragedy, Hanna began to educate himself about the most humane manner in which to hang criminals. Hanna never pulled the trap door lever himself; this was to be done by the county sheriff. He requested that his only payment be to receive the weapon the condemned man had used to commit his crime. Hanna even converted a part of his home into a museum to display the weapons and hanging memorabilia he had collected over the years. He had glass cases under which he had pieces of rope and black masks from hangings across the country. Hanna's involvement in public executions continued after Conner was hanged, and he supervised the last public execution in the United States, that of Rainey Bethea, on August 14, 1936, in Owensboro, Kentucky.

The hanging of Conner would be the first execution for Sheriff Hudson, and he was dreading it. It was going to be difficult to kick the trap that would plunge Conner to his death because of the childlike trust Conner had placed in him. (It was an unusual bond that often developed between a sheriff and his prisoner during the weeks awaiting the execution.) There were many people who envied Hudson, and some even offered him money if he would let them execute Conner. For Hudson it was a distasteful but official duty that he was not able to shirk or pass off to someone else.

Two days before his execution, Conner's brother-in-law, Ed Wade, visited Conner and shaved him. Then three formal photographs of Conner were taken by Deputy Sheriff William Joseph Perks with Conner arrayed in a new shirt and necktie, which were then displayed in the front window of the *Cairo Bulletin* newspaper office.[30] The day before his hanging, friends and family were brought to his cell, and Conner was kidding with them and laughing. Conner, still smoking heavily on the last full day of his life, once again became animated toward his visitors. He told his friends he had made his peace with God but was not yet "ready to go."[31]

Several ministers visited Conner, who as a boy had attended Sunday school in Tennessee at Trenton Colored Methodist Episcopal Church. The Reverend William H. Cole, the minister of the African Methodist Episcopal Church in Mound City, probably visited Conner the most, but he was also visited by members of the Salvation Army from Cairo, with whom Conner sang hymns and prayed. The Reverend Cole said Conner prayed often, could offer a good prayer by the time of his death, and continuously expressed regret for his actions. Conner did not drink or gamble and stated that "women had played no part in his failure to lead the right kind of life."[32] He told visitors and newspaper reporters that he attributed his "downfall" to bad male companions, such as Fred Hale, who had proposed the robbery to Conner.[33]

He advised his younger brother not to carry a gun, saying, "If I had not been carrying a gun, I would be a free man today."[34]

Conner recovered his nerve on the day of his execution and walked "game" to the scaffold on his own, just as he had promised Sheriff Hudson. Hanna stated that Hess Conner was the most composed victim he had ever seen in his vast experience of hangings.[35] He had eaten a hearty breakfast earlier, bathed, and put on a new blue serge suit provided by the sheriff. When Sheriff Hudson went to his cell to get him, Hudson asked, "Well, how are you?" Conner repeated the same question to the sheriff and then said, "I promised you I would do my part to make it easy for you. Here is my hand on it. I am not afraid and won't weaken."

In an interview with the *Pulaski Enterprise*, then edited by 21-year-old University of Illinois student George Gale Roberson, Sheriff Hudson stated, "The boy had religion; something else besides bravery was holding him up. I believe that Conner was ready to die."[36] Hudson recounted how he had offered Conner liquor, despite the fact that it was the height of Prohibition, but that the prisoner had declined, saying that since he "had religion," it was not right. Conner also told the sheriff that he was somewhat relieved he had received a death sentence rather than life imprisonment like Fred Hale, his accomplice, "Cause, Mr. Hudson, my troubles will soon be over."[37]

A fine mist was falling outside on the execution day. Two deputies walked on each side of Hess Conner to the scaffold, but they did not touch him as he made the journey of about 50 yards from his cell, across the courthouse lawn, and up the steps to the platform. His hands were cuffed together in front of him. The Reverend Cole walked with Conner and the "death party" up the scaffold and delivered a brief address from the fifth chapter of Romans:[38]

Therefore being justified by faith, we have peace with God through our Lord Jesus Christ:

By whom also we have access by faith into this grace wherein we stand, and rejoice in hope of the glory of God.

And not only so, but we glory in tribulations also: knowing that tribulation worketh patience;

And patience, experience; and experience, hope:

And hope maketh not ashamed; because the love of God is shed abroad in our hearts by the Holy Ghost which is given unto us.

For when we were yet without strength, in due time Christ died for the ungodly.

Cole added, "Man can destroy the body, but not the soul."

Waiting for Conner on the platform were Sheriff Hudson, Massac County Sheriff Osterloh "Osro" Shirk; the new Republican Pulaski County State's Attorney, Edward L. Merchant; Phil Hanna, Deputy Anderson of Karnak; and Deputy John E. Walbridge of Mounds. Stationed around the inside of the stockade were Pulaski County deputies, Alexander County deputies, and five Cairo policemen, all with riot guns in case there was trouble.

Conner was asked if he had any last words he would like to say to the assembled crowd. He said, "I wants to thank Mr. Hudson for his goodness and kindness and also his wife, and Deputy Sheriff Wilson and all the deputies. They has all been mighty good to me and I'll never forget 'em. I hopes you all will forgive me for the crime I has done." He coughed and continued, "God has forgave me and I hopes you all will."[39]

Sheriff Shirk of Metropolis then strapped Conner's arms and legs. Phil Hanna put the black hood over his head, placed the noose around his neck, and tightened it. Hanna's nod was the signal to Sheriff Hudson to kick the lever, and at 10:20 A.M. the trap was sprung. The *Cairo Bulletin* claimed that Conner's neck was broken by the fall and the noose, and "there was not a tremor or movement of the body."[40] Three physicians, Dr. William R. Wesenberg of Mound City; Dr. Otis T. Hudson of Mounds, the Pulaski County coroner and brother of the sheriff; and Dr. James Elmer Woelfle of Cairo placed their stethoscopes on Conner's chest every few seconds as he remained hanging from the rope. It took 16 minutes for his heart to stop beating, and his body hung there for 23 minutes.[41]

J. C. Wilson, father of Daisy, stood close to the scaffold to witness the hanging.[42] The *Cairo Evening Citizen* reported that he showed no emotion "other than a quick tightening of the lips as Conner shot downward thru [*sic*] the trap."[43] Other official witnesses were nine Illinois sheriffs, a coroner's jury, court attachés, and the three doctors.[44] Judge Hartwell, the sentencing judge, was supposed to attend but had sent a message that he would not be present.

No women were allowed within the stockade during the hanging, but a crowd of nearly a thousand persons gathered on the outside. Dozens of people, mostly men but a few women, could see the hanging from courthouse and jail windows. Some had cameras to record the occasion.[45] Some of the younger and stronger spectators witnessed the event from the courthouse roof, and others climbed telephone poles to get a better view. Conner's jail mates, including Henry Winter, one of the leaders of the mob that had tried to lynch the two men falsely accused, could see the hanging from their cell windows. Conner's sister, Mattie Lee Wade, went to Grand Chain to be with friends on the day of the hanging, but her husband, Ed Wade, was present.[46] While Conner hung suspended by the rope, people were allowed to come into the stockade to view the dead body. Women were allowed in now, and some of them were carrying small children in their arms and holding others by the hand.

After the spectacle was viewed by all who wanted to see it, Conner's body was taken down. Men first had to grab the rope and pull the body up so the end could be untied. His body was then slowly lowered and placed in a long basket and carried to Undertaker George Hartwell's hearse. Conner's sister, Mattie Lee Wade of Mound City, claimed the body, although the expenses of the burial were paid by Pulaski County.[47] After a funeral on Sunday, he was buried at Mounds in a now unmarked grave. Conner had given his life in payment for the crime of casually and thoughtlessly taking the life of Daisy Wilson, but no payment could ever be enough to compensate her family for their loss. After the hanging, J. C. Wilson drove despondently back to his home and store in Villa Ridge with little or no feeling of satisfaction or closure.

The experience had clearly shaken and shaped the life of Sheriff Hudson, who chose not to run for reelection in 1926 but was elected county treasurer.[48] He expressed his wish that state penitentiaries take over the job of executing prisoners and that hanging be replaced by the electric chair, which Hudson called a "death chair."[49] The sheriff was not opposed to the death penalty but believed that execution degraded both the victim and authorities while exciting the wrong kind of passions among the people. If the condemned were executed "on the quiet" by the state, local people would no longer have a role in executions. Indeed, there was a high correlation between the end of lynching in America and the assumption of capital punishment by the states.[50]

After the sheriff performed one of the 143 legal executions in the United States in 1925, he ordered the borrowed scaffold to be quickly taken down and returned to Murphysboro. The gallows would continue to make the rounds and was used a few years later in 1928 in Benton in Franklin County to hang the gangster and bootlegger Charlie Birger. His was the last public execution by hanging in Illinois.

CHAPTER ELEVEN

Lynch Mob Indictments and Trial

A S SOON AS THE INDICTMENTS against Conner and Hale were completed in July 1924, the same grand jury began hearing evidence against those involved in the mob action at Mound City.[1] Practically all of the leaders of the lynch mob that had chased Sheriff Hudson and his prisoners through the county and assembled at Mounds were known to Hudson and other officials, but the legal action centered on those leading the assault on the jail at Mound City.[2] Several witnesses gave testimony to the jury concerning the identification of men who had formed the mob outside the courthouse.[3] Since no lynching occurred, the investigation focused on "unlawful assembly," which was a misdemeanor.[4] The charges initially extended to "riot," but State's Attorney Loren Boyd believed he could not get convictions for so serious a crime, and it would have been politically damaging to have tried. Nine men were indicted as the leaders of the mob, and Judge Hartwell issued bench warrants for their arrests.[5] If convicted, the men could serve one year in jail and be fined $1,000.

The men were initially accused of disturbing the peace, refusing to disperse when ordered by the sheriff, and intending to lynch the prisoners in custody. The first indictment charged that on July 22, 1924, "being then and there members of a mob assembled for the purpose of disturbing the public peace and quiet of the neighborhood of the county jail of the aforesaid county by loud and unusual noises, offensive and tumultuous carriage, cursing, threatening, traducing, quarreling, [and] challenging to fight."[6]

The second formal accusation was for failure to disperse. It stated, "Then and there being members of a collection of individuals of more than thirty in number then and there unlawfully, riotously and tumultuously assembled in the city of Mound City in the aforesaid county with the intent to disturb the public peace, willfully and maliciously to break down, deface, destroy and take prisoners from the jail of said county, refused, on the lawful command of duly appointed and commissioned deputy sheriffs of said county then and there to disperse.[7]

The third indictment was the most serious. It charged that "on the 22nd day of July in the year of our Lord one Thousand nine hundred and twenty-four, at and in the County aforesaid being then and there members of a mob unlawfully, riotously and tumultuously assembled with the intent unlawfully to inflict injury to persons then and there charged with crime."[8]

An examination of the lives the nine men indicted, as with those in the Elco Trouble in July 1924 in Alexander County, reveals nothing out of the ordinary. They were all White, mostly poor, working-class men from Pulaski and Alexander Counties, and, typical of the time, had an eighth-grade or less education. Their average age was 32, six were married, one was a widower, and two were unmarried; four were fathers of children, and three were veterans of World War I.

Daniel Webster "Webb" Hill was born in Karnak and was 47 years old. He had a seventh-grade education and worked in the box factory in Grand Chain, but by 1920 he was devoting his full attention to farming near Karnak. The circuit court records list Hill as "Richard Roe," suggesting that his identity was not known to the grand jury or state's attorney when the indictment was written. His wife was Maude Mae Husk of Dunklin County, Missouri, who was 32 when Webb was arrested. They had four children in 1924 ranging in ages from 9 months to 11 years old.

George Charles Niemeyer was 44, a native of Metropolis, Massac County, where he completed the eighth grade. He had worked in the Grand Chain area as a farm laborer and at the box factory before moving to Cache Precinct in Johnson County by 1920 and by 1924 was living in Karnak. The circuit court records list him as "John Doe," suggesting that his identity was not known to the grand jury or state's attorney when the indictment was written. His wife was Winnie Housewright and they had four children in 1924 from ages 5 to 17.

Oscar Alexander Reed was 35 and a native of Grand Chain, where he grew up and received an eighth-grade certificate. He married Leatha Carson. When he registered for the draft in 1917, he lived in Cairo and was a locomotive fireman for the Illinois Central. In 1920 he was living in Cache Precinct, Alexander County, and was a railroad engineer. At the time of his arrest in 1924, he and his wife had two living children ages two and three.

Floyd Norman "Dutch" Galbraith was 31, a native of Villa Ridge. He moved to Cairo and found work in a sawmill as a young man. He enlisted in 1917 and served as a cook during World War I in France until his honorable discharge in 1919. He returned to Cairo to his parents' home and was a sawyer at the Chicago Mill. A member of Company K of the Illinois National Guard at Cairo at the time he allegedly joined the lynch mob, he was a widower when he was arrested and had no children.

Ora Winteroad Bradbury was 31 and a native of Newton, Jasper County, Illinois. He served in France during World War I as a wagoner in the antiaircraft artillery. He was manager of the Indian Refining Company, which had large oil tanks on the Ohio River, where petroleum was unloaded from river barges and transported by rail. He moved to Cairo about 1920 and was not married.

Mack "Fatty" Morse was 27 years old, a native of Princeton, Caldwell County, Kentucky, where he was partially raised by his grandparents. He graduated from eighth grade before leaving home. He moved to Cairo as a young man and found work at the Cairo Electric and Traction Company. After registering for the draft in 1918, he was a conductor on the interurban rail between Cairo and Mound City in 1920. His 22-year-old wife was Elsie Elva Rhymer, and they had no children in 1924.

Harry Monroe Winters was a native of Barlow, Kentucky, and 27 years old. The highest grade he completed was third grade. Before 1917 he moved to Mound City and was night watchman at the Marine Ways and Dock Company. He entered the U.S. Army in 1917 as a private, served as a military policeman in Europe, and was honorably discharged in 1919. He returned to Illinois after the war and lived in Mounds in 1920. At the time of his arrest he was married to Abbie Rose Fitzgerald and had three children aged 7 months to 3 years.

Robert W. "Rob" Staten was born in Karnak and was 23. He left school after completing the fifth grade. He was married and worked as a farm laborer on his father's farm near Mound City. He was married to Hattie Mae Smith in 1922.

Roy Vancleve Ogden was 22, a native of Henderson County, Kentucky, where he attended school through sixth grade. His parents were farmers in Ballard County, Kentucky, and he was unmarried at the time of his arrest in 1924.

Mack "Fatty" Morse and Ora W. Bradbury, both of Cairo, voluntarily surrendered to the sheriff, posted a $500 bond each, and were released.[9] They were among the leaders of the mob that organized outside the Wilson home after Sheriff Hudson left there with the two suspects and the mob followed them to Mounds and then to Mound City. They claimed they had nothing to do with the Mound City mob and that someone had given their names to the authorities because they saw them in town after troops arrived to quell the riot.[10] George Niemeyer of Karnak was the third arrested, on Monday, August 4. Floyd "Dutch" Galbraith, of Company K at Cairo, and Harry Winters, a prominent local wrestler from Urbandale, left the state as soon as they learned there were warrants for their arrest. The others were from Pulaski County and were also "dodging arrest."[11]

Sheriff Hudson was determined to bring all the lynch mob leaders to trial: "I shall not give up the hunt until everyone of the men indicted are under arrest. . . . I shall still be looking for them the day I go out of office unless they have been captured in the meantime. The search will continue as long as I am in office, and the warrants then will be turned over to my successor if I have not captured them."

It is notable that the press in Pulaski and Alexander Counties refused to justify the attempted double lynching in July 1924 as they had done on the occasion of the 1909 double lynching in Cairo of Will "Froggie" James and Henry A. Salzner. The *Pulaski Enterprise*, published in Mound City, declared there was scant sympathy for the mob and praised Sheriff Hudson for preserving the county's reputation. The newspaper argued that the basis of law was order and that the July mob had grossly defied established order.[12] The *Cairo Bulletin* stated that the Pulaski County authorities had saved their county "from a blight that is not early lived down. Their conduct assumes special merit in view of the disregard for orderly law enforcement which has been so offensively and so dangerously conspicuous in recent past—especially in Southern Illinois."[13] The writer was likely referring to the Klan War and violence in Williamson and Franklin Counties. The *Cairo Evening Citizen*, published in a town that had experienced two lynchings in one night 15 years earlier, was more to the point and stated, "Pulaski County is to be congratulated. She escaped mob rule."[14]

The three local newspapers were influential in forming and shaping public opinion of White citizens. There is, however, no evidence to show what the average White citizen thought of the members of the lynch mob or what they said in private about the attempted lynching. There is also no evidence that there was a consensus of opinion among White men in the counties. Knowing as they did, after the fact, that the men the lynch mob was intent on murdering were not guilty, there was likely little support for the attempted lynching. There were some White citizens willing to forgive the mob and rationalize the attempted murder by saying the mob had made an "honest mistake." Thus, the indicted men had sympathizers who certainly were not anxious to see them punished, and the indicted men did not fear significant trouble from the law.

Unlike the aftermath of the lynching of Froggie James in Cairo in 1909, in 1924 there was no protest by Americans of African descent in Pulaski County, at least none that appeared in the press. There was no outcry for equal justice under the law. No Black citizens were quoted in the local press at the time of the crime and punishment, but the local press assured their readers that the Black community also approved of the legal proceedings and the execution of Hess Conner.[15] It may have been because the potential lynching victims were not from Pulaski County. Jones and Brown were from Memphis, and Hale and Conner were from Cairo. Also, Black Pulaski County officers had been instrumental not only in protecting the potential victims of the lynching but of apprehending the actual criminals. This is especially true of African American Deputy James "Jim" Wilson, who rode shotgun with Sheriff Hudson when the sheriff was transporting the suspects. He also was instrumental in getting Hess Conner to confess to killing Daisy Wilson. Black leaders in Pulaski County did not take a stand to protest or publicly comment against the lynch mobs, and so it would seem that most Black people in Pulaski County were willing to accept the tepid action taken by authorities against White mob leaders.

The five men called the ring leaders by State's Attorney Boyd were still at large in August 1924. For that reason, all cases, including those against the men who had been apprehended, were continued until the October term.[16] Roy Ogden fled the state on July 23, after the indictments were handed down, and was arrested in Ballard County, Kentucky, on Wednesday, September 3, 1924.[17] He was placed in jail at Wickliffe, Kentucky, but refused to come back voluntarily to Mound City with Deputy Charles Walbridge, so a petition for requisition was filed on September 10.[18] Ogden submitted a petition to the governor that was cosigned by several hundred citizens of Ballard County, Kentucky, just across the Ohio River from Cairo. The Ogden petition declared that "the jury would be packed with negroes, who, he claimed would be prejudiced against him."[19] The governor of Kentucky, William Jason Fields, refused the request from Illinois, saying that Ogden could not get a fair trial in Pulaski County.[20] All nine indicted, except Galbraith and Ogden, were captured or had turned themselves in by October 1924.[21]

Harry Winters, feeling remorseful for his actions or just wanting the ordeal to be over, pled guilty to being involved in the attempted lynching in Mounds on the night of July 22. He was sentenced to 30 days in the county jail and a fine of one hundred dollars on the same day that Hess Conner was executed by hanging.[22] While serving his sentence in the Pulaski County jail, he witnessed the hanging of Hess Conner.[23] He was the only one of the members charged to be convicted, and that was only because he made a confession. Had he not been eager to confess, he could have been released with the others.

When the case for riot was called in October 1924, the state's attorney asked for a continuance until January 1925, at which time the newly elected state's attorney, Edward L. Merchant, would have assumed office.[24] Harry Winters, although willing to confess guilt for himself, was apparently not willing to be a witness against other accused mob leaders. Charges against Bradbury, Reed, and Morse for participating in the first mob at Mounds were dropped due to insufficient evidence in January 1925, six months after the crime.[25] The case against the others was ordered to be certified to the county court for process and trial, but no further record can be found, and they were not prosecuted.[26]

The failure to convict and punish the men in the would-be lynch mobs was typical. Even when accused men and women were lynched, it was not uncommon for people from the mob to be brazen enough to pose for photographs with the dead bodies. A merchant in Pulaski, Illinois, displayed a piece of rope in his store that he had taken as a souvenir in a lynching during the early 1900s.[27] It was very uncommon for any member of an American lynch mob to be prosecuted, and few were convicted and sentenced. From 1877 to 1950, no White individual was convicted of murder for lynching a Black person, according to a 2015 study.[28] *Lynching in America: Confronting the Legacy of Racial Terror*, a report by the Equal Justice Initiative, shows only 1 percent of lynch mob members were convicted of any criminal offense.[29] When charges were brought against lynchers, indictments were most often for disturbing the peace, unlawful assembly, or rioting. In most cases they were never even charged with any crime and remained identified as "persons unknown" in legal records. The Pulaski County case, which was for attempted lynching, shows that even when the persons were known, the system allowed them to walk away unprosecuted and unpunished if they were indeed guilty.

After the Springfield, Illinois, race riot in 1908, in which nine Black residents and seven White residents of the capital were killed, the state passed an antilynching law, but it was sometimes ignored.[30] Leonidas C. Dyer, a Missouri congressman, introduced legislation to establish lynching as a federal crime in 1918. The Dyer Bill was deemed necessary because county and state courts had failed to successfully prosecute and convict members of lynch mobs, as had happened repeatedly across the country and in Alexander and Pulaski Counties. The bill passed in the House of Representatives but due to filibusters did not come to a vote in the Senate. Not until the Emmett Till Antilynching Act was passed in the House and the Senate and was signed into law by President Joseph R. Biden on March 29, 2022, was there a national law recognizing lynching as a crime.

The obvious lesson for Americans of African descent in 1925 was that when one of them was accused of killing a White person it meant almost certain death, imprisonment, or possible lynching if they were caught—and the sheriff was not as devoted to law and order as Ira J. Hudson. Another lesson that circulated among some Black Americans was that justice meant "just us." That is, just Americans of African descent would go to prison and the gallows for capital crimes, while lynching-bent White citizens would go free or perhaps get 30 days in jail. Americans of African descent clearly held a position of second-class citizenship when it came to the criminal justice system then in place.

CHAPTER TWELVE

The Second Klan Fades from Memory

THE LAST BIG HURRAH for the national Ku Klux Klan happened on August 8, 1925, when about thirty-five thousand masked and robed Klansmen paraded down Pennsylvania Avenue in Washington, D.C.[1] Every state east of the Mississippi River was represented, but if there were any men from Alexander and Pulaski Counties present, the local press did not report it. During the second evening of the gala, an 80-foot tall and 30-foot wide cross was burned in the nation's capital as two hundred new members were initiated into the Ku Klux Klan.[2] The Klan put on a big show, but beneath the façade leaders knew the organization was in trouble. By 1925 their numbers had begun to dwindle locally, statewide, and nationally.

Klan membership diminished as members became disillusioned by repeated reports of corruption among national and state leadership. The Klan's publicity agents, Edward Young Clark, imperial wizard *pro tempore* of the Ku Klux Klan from 1915 to 1922, and Elizabeth Tyler, were largely credited with expanding Klan membership and establishing the system of payment to the Klan hierarchy. In 1919, however, in Atlanta, Georgia, the two were arrested in a hotel room together while in the possession of whisky.[3] Although national Prohibition did not go into effect until 1920, the State of Georgia had enacted a ban on alcohol in 1907, and Clark and Tyler were found in violation of state law. Clark resigned as wizard in 1921 and was later ousted, and Elizabeth Tyler left the Klan after being accused of embezzling. These incidents hampered the growth of the national organization, but new leadership assured the public that the problems had been resolved and recruitment continued. When organization efforts began in Pulaski and Alexander Counties in early 1923, the Clark–Tyler scandals were well known, but some local men were enthusiastic to join, convinced that the unethical and immoral advisors had been weeded out.

Another disastrous blow to the Klan occurred in March 1924 when Klan recruitment was robust in Pulaski and Alexander Counties. No longer in a leadership position, Edward Young Clark pleaded guilty to violating the Mann Act, a federal law that made it illegal to transport across state lines "any woman or girl for the purpose of prostitution or debauchery or for any other immoral purpose." Clark had taken a young woman from Houston, Texas, to New Orleans, Louisiana. Klan members in Pulaski and Alexander Counties followed the case, and the front page of the *Cairo Evening Citizen* published a picture of Clark in his black robe, which it stated was the first time that robe of officialdom had been photographed for publication.[4] An FBI investigation of Clark discovered that he had kept eight dollars of every ten dollars he had collected in initiation fees and made more by selling Klan regalia. When he was thrown out of the Klan in January 1924, the income of the Klan was reputed to have been $12 million.

Other scandals also plagued the Klan leadership and hampered organizers. David Curtis Stephenson, Indiana grand dragon, was in charge of recruitment in Indiana and Illinois and gained a reputation as a heavy drinker and womanizer.[5] Imperial Wizard Hiram Evans tried to oust him after they disagreed about the distribution of membership fees, but he refused to leave. Stephenson established an autonomous rival Klan organization in September 1923 independent of the national organization. After he kidnapped, raped, beat, and murdered 29-year-old Madge Oberholtzer in March 1925, he was convicted and sentenced to life in prison on November 16, 1925.[6] By this time the local klaverns in Pulaski and Alexander Counties, as well as others across the Midwest, were losing members and beginning to fold.

The Illinois Ku Klux Klan was in chaos because of internal bickering among state leaders. Charles D. McGehee, grand dragon of 47 southern Illinois counties, was removed in September 1923 and soon was terminated as the titan of the Illinois District by Charles G. Palmer, grand dragon of the Klan of Illinois.[7] McGehee was removed from state leadership but became a national lecturer for the Ku Klux Klan and resided in Cairo in 1924.[8] His instrumental work in organizing the Klan in Alexander County was mostly after his removal as an Illinois grand dragon.[9]

In southern Illinois the most notorious and best known leader associated with the Ku Klux Klan was S. Glenn Young, who also suffered legal battles and dishonor. He was fired from the Prohibition Unit of the Treasury Department in December 1920, a month after he killed Luke Vukovic, an alleged bootlegger, during a raid near Granite City in Madison County.[10] He was acquitted of murder by a Madison County jury but dismissed as a federal officer for being "of a belligerent nature, prone to make threats of violence," and the investigators concluded that "the evidence overwhelmingly shows Agent Young to be a glaring disgrace to the service."[11] After his dismissal, Young became a freelance prohibition investigator in southern Illinois. Some voiced disapproval after he confiscated a roulette wheel, gambling chips, and $157.50 in cash in a raid at Tamms and refused to turn them over to local authorities.[12] An internal investigation also revealed that Young had frequently checked into hotels with his mistress, and his wife divorced him for cruelty and lack of support in July 1921 while he was under investigation by the Treasury Department.

Young was paid several thousand dollars to stop illegal alcohol trafficking, and his work led to the Klan War from January 1924 to April 1926 in which 20 people were killed in Williamson County.[13] Problems of violence became so severe that in January 1924, National Guard troops, including Company K from Cairo, were sent into Williamson to maintain order and had to be sent there four more times before order was completely restored.[14] Young was removed as kleagle of the East St. Louis Ku Klux Klan in July 1924 by Grand Titan Charles G. Palmer.[15] The violence gained national media attention and condemnation of the Illinois Klan—and yet men joined the Klan in Alexander and Pulaski Counties. They were told that the press was spreading lies about the Ku Klux Klan in Williamson County and ignoring what they called the good work being done there. Young was killed in a shootout in Herrin with Williamson County Deputy Ora Thomas on January 24, 1925. As the Klan became increasingly associated with violence outside the law, members dropped out and chose not to renew their membership.[16] When federal agents began to clean up criminal bootlegging activities in Alexander County in 1927 and 1928, the Klan was in no way involved.

Members did not generally stay with the Second Ku Klux Klan of the 1920s for long. In January 1923, the Ku Klux Klan in East St. Louis claimed a membership of 5,000 but by the end of the year had only 850 dues-paying members. After joining the Klan amidst the hype of initiation, one member said that the only Klan activity was bringing in new members. The whole organization came to be seen as a pyramid scheme, where Klansmen could make money by recruiting new members. For example, to advance to second-degree Klansman, one had to recruit at least one new dues-paying member.[17]

The moral failings, hypocrisy, and corruption of national and state Klan leaders caused many members to drop from the membership rolls of local klaverns. As David Chalmers wrote in his history of the Ku Klux Klan, "The godly came to realize that the Klan was not."[18] Few if any were willing to admit that they had been hoodwinked by Klan leaders, who had played on their racist sentiments and fears to get into their pockets in order to line their own with dues collection and the selling of Klan regalia and materials. Even more difficult to admit was the role Christian Protestant ministers, many of whom had given moral endorsement to the Klan, had played in the scheme.

Klaverns in Pulaski and Alexander Counties were small and politically weak. Most White men there did not join the Klan. Native-born White males with native-born parents were the recruiting base for the Klan. In 1920 there were 4,435 of them, comprising 18.5 percent of the population in Alexander County, and 2,352, or 16 percent of the population in Pulaski County.[19] It is unknown how many actually joined the Ku Klux Klan in the two counties. In Williamson County, where the Klan was much stronger and more active, Masatomo Ayabe, in his history of the Klan movement in that county, with a population of about fifty-five thousand, determined from names in local press accounts and court records that they numbered from three hundred to four hundred members there.[20] No membership rolls exist, but it is likely their numbers would have been about the same in Alexander and Pulaski Counties, which in 1924 had a combined population of about thirty-eight thousand.

The Second Ku Klux Klan was down to about 350,000 members in 1927 from its peak of two to five million a few years earlier.[21] The final blow was the ailing economy. The Great Depression that officially began in 1929 and lasted through the 1930s "killed the Klan in Illinois" according to an Illinois legislative investigation in 1975.[22] Most people, especially in rural counties of southern Illinois, did not have spare money to join or retain membership in the Klan. When it came time to renew their dues, members increasingly weighed the decision and simply did not see the point in membership, although most still believed in White supremacy.

The influence of the local kleagle, or organizer, Forest Hazel Moreland waned after the lynching incidents at Mounds and Mound City. With fewer members paying dues, his income from the Klan was cut drastically, and he had to find other work to support his family. Moreland left Pulaski County within the next few years and moved to Clewiston, Florida, where he worked on a sugarcane farm and was a deputy sheriff.[23] By 1940, when Moreland returned to Illinois to live in Metropolis, the Second Ku Klux Klan had disappeared from the region.

Another local Klan leader, the Reverend William P. Anderson, delivered his farewell sermon to the First Christian Church in Cairo on November 2, 1924. He left Cairo to accept a pastorate of a new church in West Palm Beach, Florida, but delivered a scathing address from the pulpit before his exodus.[24] He said his efforts to "clean up" Cairo and rid it of corruption had been misunderstood by many in the congregation, and he blamed them and other "church people" for not standing up to corruption in the city. "Your city is infested with crooks from all parts of the country and good folks have to suffer for that," he said. The factories in town, he complained, only paid "surviving wages." He then spoke of what he called "the negro problem." Anderson preached segregation and said, "The negroes should have their own community in which to live." He left the next day and never returned to Cairo.[25]

The last mention in the local press of a meeting of the Second Ku Klux Klan in Pulaski County was June 25, 1924. The last notice in Alexander County was about a meeting in Cairo in August 1924. Local klaverns existed for a brief time after the media hype and attention disappeared, but they had gone into hiding and their activities were no longer being reported in the county newspapers. The lynch mobs in Pulaski County in the summer of 1924, which almost murdered two innocent men, may have opened the eyes of some to what end the Klan's racist rhetoric could lead, but more likely the people had just moved on and were trying to forget that event and disassociate themselves and their communities from it. They were putting the sheet over the past and their memories of it.

Lillian Nesbitt Butler recalled in her book, *Living in Cache Bottom*, seeing a cross burning in rural Pulaski, Illinois, in the 1920s when she was a child and stated, "It was a sight for the community to witness."[26] She wrote, "It was near the home of a black woman who was accused of pushing a white woman off the street in Pulaski." Butler stated that she and her family could easily identify some of the Klansmen as local Pulaski men even though they were disguised by their white robes and hoods, and she said, "Everyone was shocked to know that his neighbor could be a 'K. K. K.'"[27] This is the last record the authors found of the Second Ku Klux Klan or Klan activities in Pulaski and Alexander Counties.

The Ku Klux Klan was short-lived in Pulaski and Alexander Counties, lasting only a few years, but the damage that small minority of citizens did in sanctioning and exposing the racism of many residents had a long-term effect in furthering distrust among racial groups. Some of the Klansmen may have gotten caught up in the moment and joined the Klan for what they saw as the fun involved, but the damage they caused by joining an organization supporting White supremacy was destructive to the region. One former Klansman ironically recalled, "We talked only about 'true Americanism'— never said or did anything against anybody, but the newspapers were full of stories about disturbances. . . . So I quit because I didn't want people to think I was a racist or bigot."[28]

Just because the Klan had begun to disappear for the second time in southern Illinois during the mid-1920s does not mean that racist attitudes faded or even subsided. On February 26, 1925, Sheriff Ira J. Hudson raided the Wind Blew Inn on Main Street in Mound City on a tip that an interracial couple had checked in there. When the sheriff and his deputies had the door to the room opened, they discovered Bertie Manley, a White woman, in bed with Matt Williams, a Black man. The *Pulaski Enterprise* reported the incident and said the sheriff "caught the pair red handed."[29] Manley and Williams were placed in the county jail, and the next day the woman pled guilty before Judge Charles S. Miller, who the previous year had been one of the public defendants of Hess Conner. Manley was fined $300 and sentenced to six months in jail. Williams received a lighter sentence of 70 days but was sent to the new Vandalia penitentiary, a prison farm that housed misdemeanor offenders.[30] And White supremacy continued without the Klan.

People use the past to celebrate accomplishments and achievements, but not all history is a celebration. Sometimes research reveals an account of the past that has been forgotten because it was not seen as significant or maybe was intentionally swept under the rug. Most communities, families, and individuals have skeletons in their closets they would prefer future generations not discover or talk about. History can sometimes be a source of shame and embarrassment to later generations and a source of pain to others, making both reluctant to confront the past. Such is the history of the Second Ku Klux Klan in Pulaski and Alexander Counties. When we pull the sheets off the past we always discover the weaknesses of humanity underneath. It can be painful to remember and acknowledge past events, but it is more dangerous if we allow ourselves to forget.

NOTES

BIBLIOGRAPHY

INDEX

NOTES

Prologue

1. Isaac Edward "Ed" Lee (1861–1932) led the Marion Law Enforcement League and testified on behalf of Carl Neilson, exalted cyclops of Herrin Buckhorn Klan, who had been accused of taking money during a Klan raid on Jefferson Hotel Bar in Herrin on January 7, 1924.

2. Dexter, *History of Beech Grove Church*, 110; "Minister against Injustice," *The Republic*, April 23, 2016.

Introduction

1. Berg, *Popular Justice*, 156. Pulaski County also carried out one of the last public hangings in the state. Thus, this botched robbery of almost a hundred years ago is also related to the drastic rise in American capital punishment in the 1920s (Rushdy, *American Lynching*, 69–93). Michael Pfeifer argues that there was a high correlation between the decline of American lynching in the 1920s and the rapid rise of state-sanctioned executions in the Midwest (Pfeifer, *Rough Justice*, 149).

2. In 2023 there are about 5,065 people in the county, making Pulaski the seventh smallest county in the State of Illinois (https://www.census.gov/population/cencounts/i1190090.txt). The population of Pulaski County has surpassed that of Alexander according to the 2020 Census, and Alexander is the fifth least populated county in Illinois with 5,030 residents in 2023.

3. Wall, Shawnee History Project, 21–23.

4. Wall, 21–22.

5. Moyers, *Brief History of Pulaski County*, unnumbered pages.

6. "R. W. England Dies," *Pulaski Enterprise*, April 5, 1967.

7. Obituary of John Carr Steele, *Cairo Evening Citizen*, April 19, 1937; "Well-Known Negro of Mound City Dies," *Mounds Independent*, April 23, 1937.

8. "From Slave to Teacher," *Mounds Independent*, March 31, 1939.

9. Gardner, *Up from Slavery*, 33.

10. Obituary of Hugo Chambliss, *Cairo Evening Citizen*, July 26, 1971; Obituary of Hugo Chambliss, *Pulaski Enterprise*, August 4, 1971.

11. *Pulaski County Illinois 1819–1987*.

12. Carlson, "Black Migration," 38.

13. "The Mound City Lynching," *Cairo Bulletin*, July 7, 1883.

14. "The Murder on the Train," *Cairo Argus and Mound City Journal*, July 7, 1883.

15. "Death on the Drop: Mound City, Illinois, Reports a Lynching Sensation," *Daily Journal and Republican*, July 7, 1883.

16. "Strangled: Mound City, Ill., the Scene of a Quiet but Satisfactory Lynching," *Chicago Tribune*, July 7, 1883.

17. Perrin, *A History of Alexander*, 558–560.

18. "Speedy Justice: Swift Vengeance Meted out to an African Murderer at Mound City, Ill.," *Daily Freeman*, July 12, 1883; Perrin, *A History of Alexander*, 560.

19. "Murder on the Train."

20. "Murder on the Train."

21. "Local News," *Cairo Bulletin*, July 8, 1883.

22. "Death on the Drop," *Freeport Journal Standard*, July 7, 1883; "The Mound City Lynching," *Cairo Bulletin*.

23. "The Mound City Lynching," *Decatur Daily Republic*, July 9, 1883; "General Local Items," *Cairo Bulletin*, July 8, 1883.

24. "Famous Trials" (website), accessed April 19, 2020.

25. "Silent Avengers," *St. Louis Post Dispatch*, July 7, 1883; "Strangled"; "The Mound City Lynching," *Chicago Tribune*, July 8, 1883; "Howard Hanged," *Tennessean*, July 7, 1883; "The Hanging of Nelson Howard," *Sun*, July 9, 1883.

26. "The Mound City Lynching," *Chicago Tribune*.

27. "The Mound City Lynching," *Decatur Daily Republic*.

28. "The Killing of Will Painter," *Cairo Evening Citizen*, March 12, 1887. Painter was killed in 1887 by Mr. Moll, a political rival to be Mound City marshal.

29. "General Local Items."

30. "General Local Items."

31. "Negroes Obtained Only 25 Cents in Wilson Robbery," *Cairo Evening Citizen*, January 16, 1925.

32. "Bent on Lynching Chase Murderers of White Girl Miles," *Daily Free Press*, July 22, 1924.

33. Berg, *Popular Justice*, 156.

34. Berg, 156; McWhirter, *Red Summer*, 175–177. The arrival of the National Guard was usually enough to protect the prisoners, but every officer and man of a Mayfield, Kentucky, militia unit chose to resign because they were called out to protect Allen Mathis, a Black man who had been accused of raping a 22-year-old White woman, Ethel McClain ("Tried and Hanged in an Hour," *San Francisco Call*,

August 1, 1906). Mathis was tried, convicted, and hanged in Mayfield only 50 minutes after he arrived in town, "while the largest and wildest mob in the history of the south looked on and shouted its approval. When pronounced dead, members of the mob, headed by a brass band playing 'There Will Be a Hot Time in the Old Town Tonight,' paraded through the streets carrying the dead negro in an open coffin" ("Speedy Justice Meted Out to Negro Brute amid Cheers from Enraged Mob," *Cairo Bulletin*, August 1, 1906).

35. Wall, Shawnee History Project, 28–30.

36. "The Cairo Lynchers Foiled," *Fort Wayne Journal Gazette*, November 18, 1909; "James Did Not Make Confession," *Cairo Evening Citizen*, November 11, 1909; "Frenzied Mob Are Cowed by Soldiers," *Waterloo Courier*, November 12, 1909.

37. See McWhirter, *Red Summer*.

38. Wade, *Fiery Cross*, 170.

39. "Police Sergeant French Murdered in Cold Blood by Pulaski Co. Sheriff," *Daily Free Press*, December 3, 1910.

40. Pegram, *One Hundred Percent*, 3.

41. Wall, Shawnee History Project, 1.

42. McWhirter, *Red Summer*, 160.

43. McVeigh, *Rise of the Ku Klux Klan*, 37.

44. Pegram, *One Hundred Percent*, 6.

45. "Fraser Elected Sheriff by over 1,100 Majority," *Cairo Evening Citizen*, November 9, 1910.

46. Wheeler, "Together in Egypt," 126.

47. "Cairo and the County," *Cairo Bulletin*, October 31, 1910; "Effect of Nellis' Defeat," November 5, 1910.

48. Wheeler, "Together in Egypt," 128.

49. "City News in Brief," *Cairo Bulletin*, October 31, 1910.

50. "Alex S. Fraser for Sheriff Elected by 1,400 Majority," *Cairo Bulletin*, November 9, 1910.

51. "Rebuke to Cairo's Sheriff," *Chicago Tribune*, November 9, 1910.

52. "Rebuke to Cairo's Sheriff"; "Capt. Greaney to Be Deputy Sheriff," *Daily Free Press*.

53. Beadles, *Stained with Blood*, 21.

54. Loewen, *Sundown Towns*, 513; Lantz, *A Community in Search of Itself,* 139–140.

55. Wheeler, "Together in Egypt," 128.

56. When John A. Beadles was working as a Comprehensive Employment and Training Act (CETA) supervisor in 1975–76, two of the three county commissioners were Republicans. All of the other county officers were Republicans until the 1976 elections.

57. See *Pulaski Enterprise*, July 25–August 1, 1924, and *Cairo Bulletin and Cairo Evening Citizen* for the same period.

58. "Cairo Negro Sentenced to Hang for Slaying Miss Daisy Wilson," *Pulaski Enterprise*, August 1, 1924.

1. The Mythical Klan and Rumors of Its Second Coming

1. "The Ku-Klux Klan," *Cairo Evening Citizen*, April 16, 1906.
2. "The Ku Klux Klan," *Cairo Bulletin*, April 15, 1906.
3. "At the Opera House," *Cairo Bulletin*, January 30, 1904.
4. "Last Night's Lecture by Rev. Thomas Dixon, Jr., at the Opera House Was a Rare Treat," *Cairo Bulletin*, February 4, 1904.
5. "At the Cairo Opera House," *Cairo Bulletin*, January 31, 1904.
6. "At Cairo Opera House," *Cairo Bulletin*, February 2, 1904.
7. "Last Night's Lecture."
8. "The Clansman," *Cairo Bulletin*, January 13, 1907.
9. Inscore, "The Clansman," 139–161.
10. Dixon, *Leopard's Spots*, 5.
11. Dixon, 126.
12. Dixon, 151,
13. Dixon, 442.
14. Dixon, *Clansman*, n.p.
15. Dixon, 205.
16. Dixon, 290.
17. Dixon, 374.
18. Dixon, *Traitor*, 53–54.
19. Dixon, 109.
20. Dixon, 305.
21. "The Ku Klux Klan—Some Talk That Negroes Will Try to Prevent Presentation of This Sensational Play," *Cairo Bulletin*, April 20, 1906.
22. "Klu Klux Klan—Some Talk."
23. "The Clansman," *Cairo Bulletin*, January 20, 1907.
24. The railroads included the Iron Mountain, Big Four, Mobile and Ohio, St. Louis–San Francisco, Illinois Central, St. Louis Southwestern, Nashville, Chattanooga and St. Louis, and Cairo and Thebes ("Cairo Is Not a Dead Town," *St. Louis Lumberman*, November 9, 1910).
25. "Klu Klux Klan Bill for Tonight," *Cairo Evening Citizen*, April 4, 1907.
26. "Will Present the Klu Klux Klan," *Cairo Bulletin*, April 4, 1907.
27. "The Clansman' Coming to Cairo," *Cairo Evening Citizen*, January 9, 1907.

28. "Ku Klux on Stage," *Cairo Bulletin*, January 14, 1907.

29. "Crowded from Pit to Dome," *Cairo Bulletin*, January 22, 1907.

30. "Crowded from Pit to Dome." It was noted that 40 members of the audience were from Wickliffe, Kentucky.

31. "Negroes Protest against 'Clansman,'" *Cairo Evening Citizen*, January 18, 1907.

32. "Barlow Minstrels," *Cairo Bulletin*, October 22, 1905; "Black-Faced Minstrels Performing in Cairo," *Cairo Bulletin*, December 12, 1906; "Big Minstrel Show Coming," *Cairo Bulletin*, March 2, 1907; "The Best Home Talent Minstrel Show Ever Given," *Cairo Bulletin*, January 20, 1914; "The 'Dandy Dixie' Minstrels," *Cairo Bulletin*, March 13, 1907; and numerous other references.

33. "Elks Minstrels a Huge Success—Local Entertainers in Role of Black Faced Comedians," *Cairo Bulletin*, April 25, 1905.

34. "'The Clansman' Tabooed. Macon Mayor's Order Results from Race Riots at Atlanta," *Washington Post*, September 25, 1906, https://blackthen.com/today-in-1906-thousands-of-blacks-protested-against-the-clansman-stage-play-in-philadelphia/.

35. "Negroes Protest to Mayor and Chief of Police against Production of 'The Clansman' at Cairo Opera House," *Cairo Bulletin*, January 18, 1907.

36. "The Clansman," *Cairo Bulletin*, April 22, 1907.

37. "Negroes at Cairo," *Cairo Bulletin*, December 6, 1905.

38. Dr. Liston D. Bass was the son of Dr. Thomas Randolph Bass and Mary Ann Carter and was born in 1854 in South Carolina, where his family enslaved 12 people before the Civil War, according to the 1860 slave schedule of Marion, South Carolina. Rev. Bass left Cairo to accept the pastorate of East St. Louis First Baptist Church but was forced to resign in September 1908 after preaching several sensational sermons stating women should not work in an office with men, should not let men kiss them before they were married, and that hired girls should not attend church ("Forced to Resign His Pastorate," *Cairo Bulletin*, September 19, 1908).

39. "Praise from Noted Critic," *Cairo Bulletin*, September 13, 1907.

40. "Police Capture a Negro Murderer," *Cairo Evening Citizen*, January 21, 1905.

41. "Dying Negress and White Youth Had a Suicide Compact," *Cairo Bulletin*, February 20, 1905.

42. "New Evidence Found against the Negro," *Cairo Bulletin*, April 20, 1905

43. "Illinois Central Flagman Killed by Negro," *Cairo Evening Citizen*, May 10, 1905.

44. "Negro Burglar Shot Down by Ullin Storekeeper," *Cairo Bulletin*, May 10, 1905.

45. "Wade Hampton Probably Fatally Wounded by Two Negroes," *Cairo Evening Citizen*, May 31, 1905.

46. "Negroes Who Make Business of Peddling Cocaine Are Fined," *Cairo Bulletin*, June 3, 1905.

47. "Slashed His Neck—Cairo's New Pitcher Victim of Negro's Assault—Was Walking Downtown with Friends When Negro Stuck Knife in His Throat," *Cairo Bulletin*, July 11 1905.

48. "Killed by a Negro—Shot Down Trying to Arrest a Black Bandit," *Cairo Bulletin*, July 16, 1905.

49. "Jim Caruthers Perhaps Fatally Cut by Negro," *Cairo Evening Citizen*, July 20, 1905.

50. "Negro Assaulted Young White Girl," *Cairo Bulletin*, July 24, 1905.

51. "Was Shot by Negroes," *Cairo Bulletin*, July 29, 1905.

52. "Negro Held for Woman's Murder," *Cairo Bulletin*, August 24, 1905.

53. "Darky Who Shot at Darky and Killed White Man Given Light Sentence," *Cairo Evening Citizen*, October 20, 1905.

54. "Negro Held for Murder of White Man," *Cairo Evening Citizen*, October 25, 1905.

55. "Young Lady Attacked on Prominent Street by Black Highwayman," *Cairo Bulletin*, November 7, 1905.

56. "Negroes of Cairo Are the Worst of Any City in the Union," *Cairo Bulletin*, December 6, 1905.

57. "Brave Teacher Kills a Negro," *Cairo Bulletin*, December 17, 1905.

58. "Mob Formed to Hang Negro Who Killed White Man,," *Cairo Evening Citizen*, December 26, 1905.

59. "Negro Kills Himself to Escape Lynching," *Cairo Evening Citizen*, December 27, 1905.

60. "Caused by Hoodlums Was the Race Trouble at Thebes," *Cairo Citizen*, July 19, 1900. The racist sentiment continued for decades. In a correspondence with Darrel Dexter, Louise Ogg, librarian for many years at Cairo Public Library, wrote, "Sometime see if you can find anyone else but me who remembers the sign on the outskirts of Thebes that said, 'N——— Don't Let the Sun Set on You in This Town.'"

61. "Thebes Lynchers," *Cairo Evening Citizen*, December 28, 1903.

62. *Daily Telegram's* Cairo City Directory for 1904.

63. "Indicted by Grand Jury," *Cairo Bulletin*, July 10, 1907.

64. Mary C. Daniels and Cornelius F. Bettis were married on July 29, 1885, in Cairo, Illinois.

65. "Grand Jury Asked to Indict Men," *Cairo Bulletin*, July 10, 1907.

66. "Park Is Closed at Mound City," *Cairo Bulletin*, August 20, 1907. The park commissioners were John Henry Hillerich, Edward Kelly, George Betts, and the Reverend Isaac A. Humberd, the Congregational minister in Mound City.

67. "Night Riders Appear in Johnson County," *Cairo Evening Citizen*, May 27, 1908.

68. The earliest historian to call the era the nadir of race relations was Logan (*Negro in American Life*).

2. Memories of the First Klan

1. Chalmers, *Hooded Americanism*, 10.

2. Chalmers, 20.

3. "A Ku Klux Sensation," *Cairo Daily Democrat*, July 20, 1868.

4. "A Ku Klux Excitement in Mound City," *Cairo Daily Democrat*, September 13, 1868.

5. "Reported Deaths of Messrs. Frick and Reichert," *Cairo Daily Democrat*, August 19, 1868.

6. "K. K. K." *Cairo Daily Bulletin*, June 20, 1874.

7. "Thebes," *Cairo Daily Bulletin*, May 6, 1874.

8. "The Other Side: A. L. Smith Makes a Statement Regarding the Row at Thebes," *Cairo Daily Bulletin*, Thursday, May 7, 1874.

9. "Ku Klux," *Cairo Daily Bulletin*, June 7, 1874.

10. Erwin, *Bloody Vendetta*, 66; "Illinois K. K. K.," *Illinois State Journal*, August 28, 1875.

11. "The Ku Klux of Egypt," *Cairo Daily Bulletin*, January 24, 1875.

12. "More Ku Klux," *Cairo Daily Bulletin*, February 2, 1875.

13. Sneed, *Ghost Towns*, 30.

14. "The Williamson County Outrage," *Cairo Daily Bulletin*, May 7, 1872.

15. "K. K. K. Illinois the Last Ditch of the Death's Head and Bloody Bones," *Chicago Daily Tribune*, August 19, 1875.

16. Hall, "Ku Klux Klan," 366. The name Golden Ring Klan is reminiscent of the Knights of the Golden Circle, which was active during the Civil War.

17. "The Trial," *Cairo Daily Bulletin*, December 12, 1872.

18. Erwin, *Bloody Vendetta*, 31–32; "K. K. K. Illinois the Last Ditch."

19. "Egypt's Curse," *Cairo Daily Bulletin*, August 20, 1875.

20. "The Ku-Klux Cases," *Cairo Daily Bulletin*, January 22, 1873. A search was made of records at the Chicago branch of the National Archives, but no federal court records pertaining to the trial have survived.

21. "The First of the Williamson County Ku-Klux Cases," *Cairo Daily Bulletin*, February 19, 1874; "K. K. K. Illinois the Last Ditch."

22. "Lawlessness: A New Phase in the Present Shame of the State of Illinois," *Chicago Daily Tribune*, August 18, 1875; "At Last! The Tables Turned on the Illinois Kuklux," *Cairo Daily Bulletin*, August 19, 1875.

23. "The Ku-Klux," *Cairo Daily Bulletin*, September 5, 1875. The organization of the first three militia companies in Williamson County began on August 17, 1875 (Raines, "Ku Klux Klan," 36).

24. Hall, "Ku Klux Klan," 367.

25. "Given Away: Duckworth, The Ku Klux, Turns State's Evidence," *Cairo Daily Bulletin*, August 31, 1875. A correspondent from Springfield reported on August 20, 1875, that 7 of the 14 men had been arrested and that one named Summers had died (*Daily Argus*, August 21, 1875).

26. "The Golden Ring," *Cairo Daily Bulletin*, September 1, 1875; "The Franklin Ku Klux," *Cairo Daily Bulletin*, September 1, 1875; "Given Away." Neal's securities for his $2,000 bail bond were his brothers, Jeremiah Neal and Thomas Neal. In all, according to Raines, 45 Franklin County men were arrested for being Klansmen. See also "The Ku Klux," *Cairo Daily Bulletin*, September 5, 1875; "The Illinois Ku Klux," *Chicago Daily Tribune*, August 29, 1875; *Marion Monitor*, September 16, 1875; "Illinois Ku Klux," *St. Louis Republican*, August 28, 1875.

27. "Illinois Ku-Klux," *Cairo Daily Bulletin*, August 27, 1875.

28. Raines, "Ku Klux Klan," 36; "Trial of the Ku-Klux," *DuQuoin Tribune*, January 20, 1876; "Williamson County Crime," *Illinois State Journal*, January 19, 1876.

29. He also named Jim O'Brien, Wash Allen, a man named Ditch, and three others as members of the Klan.

30. Raines, "Ku Klux Klan," 38; "Lawlessness"; "Trial of the Ku-Klux."

31. "The Williamson and Jackson County Outlaws," *Inter-Ocean*, August 16, 1875.

32. "The Illinois Trouble," *Cairo Daily Bulletin*, August 22, 1875.

33. "Dark and Bloody Ground: Ku Klux in Hardin County," *Cairo Daily Bulletin*, July 13, 1879.

34. "Our Own K. K. K.," *Carbondale New Era*, May 4, 1872. The two members who testified against the others were Frank Hardin and Benjamin Z. Jenkins.

35. "Bloody Hardin," *Cairo Daily Bulletin*, July 16, 1879.

36. "Logan Belt," *Cairo Daily Bulletin*, July 30, 1879. Logan Belt was released from prison early and was shot dead three miles north of Cave-in-Rock in June 1887 ("Logan Belt," *Cairo Citizen*, June 16, 1887).

37. "Capt. Belt," *Cairo Daily Bulletin*, July 30, 1879.

38. Hall, "Ku Klux Klan," 370.

39. Hall, 269–270.

40. "Their Politics," *Cairo Bulletin*, September 14, 1875.

41. "Outrages in Southern Illinois," *Cairo Daily Bulletin*, October 8, 1874.

42. "Outrages in Southern Illinois."

43. "Attention," *Cairo Daily Bulletin*, November 19, 1874.

44. "Our Kingdom for a Dead N—— in Williamson County," *Cairo Daily Bulletin*, August 4, 1875.

3. The Second Coming of the Klan

1. McVeigh, *Rise of the Ku Klux Klan*, 19.
2. "The Ku Klux Kreed," *Kloran*, 2.
3. Gordon, *Second Coming*, 14.
4. Gordon, 15.
5. McVeigh, *Rise of the Ku Klux Klan*, 25.
6. Gordon, *Second Coming*, 64.
7. "Socialist Leader Entertained Crowd—Eugene V. Debs Attentively Listened to at Opera House Last Night," *Cairo Citizen*, March 20, 1906; "Eugene V. Debs," *Pulaski Enterprise*, March 9, 1906.
8. "Wizard Says Klan Isn't Anti-Anything," *New York Herald*, October 12, 1921.
9. Ayabe, "Ku Klux Klan Movement," 114.
10. "House Scores in Ku Klux Klan," *Broad Ax*, June 18, 1921.
11. Rep. Turner also sponsored a bill to provide $35,000 for the investigation of bomb throwing (Williams, *Political Empowerment*).
12. "House Scores."
13. McAndrew, "History: The 1920s."
14. Chalmers, *Hooded Americanism*, 184.
15. Chalmers, 184.
16. Ayabe, "Ku Klux Klan Movement," 1.
17. McVeigh, *Rise of the Ku Klux Klan*, 187.
18. Ayabe, "Ku Klux Klan Movement," 115.
19. "Klan Enters Church in Two Egypt Towns," *Cairo Evening Citizen*, February 26, 1923.
20. Angle, *Bloody Williamson*, 135.
21. "Du Quoin Visited by Klan," *Jonesboro Gazette*, August 17, 1923.
22. "K. K. K. in Gigantic Meeting," *Jonesboro Gazette*, August 24, 1923.
23. Galligan, *In Bloody Williamson*, 20.
24. "Another Notch on Revolver of Daring Officer," *Cairo Evening Citizen*, October 24, 1923.
25. Gordon, *Second Coming*, 27.
26. Galligan, *In Bloody Williamson*, 21.
27. Ayabe, "Ku Kluxers," 73–100.
28. McAndrew, "History: The 1920s."

4. Pulaski and Alexander Counties in 1923

1. *Fourteenth Census of the United States*, 155.

2. *Cairo Illinois City Directory*.

3. Wall, Shawnee History Project, 6.

4. "Illinois Roads Must Have No 'Jim Crow' Cars," *Cairo Bulletin*, July 11, 1914. In 1953, John A. Beadles and his father rode the GM&O "Little Rebel" from Cairo to St. Louis. The segregated White cars had few White passengers, but the two rear cars were packed with Black people because Missouri was then a segregated state.

5. Miami Powder Company opened the dynamite plant in 1906. It was replaced by Aetna Powder Company and then Hercules Powder Company.

6. The official population of Pulaski County was 14,629 in 1920 and 14,834 in 1930 (*Fifteenth Census of the United States*).

7. The official "Negro" population of Pulaski County was 4,989 in 1920 and 4,946 in 1930 (*Fifteenth Census of the United States*).

8. The official population of Alexander County was 23,980 in 1920 and 22,542 in 1930 (*Fifteenth Census of the United States*).

9. The 1930 census listed two Americans of African descent living in Thebes Precinct, Abe and Mary McGee, farm laborers.

10. The official "Negro" population of Alexander County was 6,436 in 1920 and 6,591 in 1930 (*Fifteenth Census of the United States*).

11. "Cairo Takes Hope," *Pantograph*, April 1, 1913.

12. "Cairo Is Passing Crisis of Flood," *Decatur Herald*, April 6, 1913.

13. "Prices Received for Corn."

14. "Convict Tells of Protection Given Him Here," *Cairo Evening Citizen and Cairo Bulletin*, December 11, 1928. Hugo Chambliss was bondsman for Carridine Dewey Bryant and Gaither Moore when they were arrested for running a still in Alexander County. When they refused to pay their $4,000 fine, Chambliss had to forfeit $1,500 to the federal court. He testified that Sheriff Leslie B. Roche of Alexander County had agreed to indemnify him for any loss and actually repaid him the $1,500.

15. "Says Sheriff Sold Mule for $15 a Gallon," *Cairo Evening Citizen and Cairo Bulletin*, December 12, 1928.

16. Sheriff Leslie B. Roche pleaded guilty and was sentenced to a year and a day in the federal penitentiary at Leavenworth, Kansas, and a $5,000 fine ("Sheriff Goes to Pen," *Jonesboro Gazette*, December 21, 1928; "Roche Is Given Year in Prison," *Cairo Evening Citizen and Cairo Bulletin*, December 13, 1928). Alexander County Deputy Ernest Rink was sentenced to one year and one day in prison and a $3,000 fine, and Deputy Herbert P. Reddix was given six months in jail and a $500 fine. Charges were dropped against Deputy Joseph Mulham. Charges against other Alexander County residents included operating a still; transporting liquor; delivering whisky

to a polling place; selling whisky; being a roadhouse bartender; keeping a saloon; operating slot machines; selling barrels, sugar, and other bootleg supplies with knowledge of their use; manufacturing stills; and extorting ("Gateway Inn Is Padlocked," *Cairo Evening Citizen and Cairo Bulletin*, December 5, 1928).

17. "News from Our Neighbors," *Cairo Bulletin*, November 8, 1907. About 25 saloons closed in Pulaski County in 1907 after the election: five in Mound City, eight in Mounds, two in Pulaski, three in Grand Chain, one in Olmsted, and two in Ullin. Only the two saloons in Wetaug remained legally opened ("Saloons Going Out of Business," *Cairo Bulletin*, November 8, 1907).

18. Lantz, *A Community in Search*, 75.

19. In 1918, the last year before Prohibition became law, Cairo received $55,736 from saloon licenses (Lantz, 79).

20. Sutherland, *Then Cometh the Devil*, 379–387.

21. Butler, *Living in Cache Bottom*, 183. She stated that students of African descent who lived in the Pulaski and Ullin areas were bused to Sandusky, which was in the Tamms school district, and the Pulaski-Ullin District had to pay their tuition. In 1932 the district began busing Black students to Mounds or Mound City for high school because tuition was cheaper.

22. "Wetaug News," *Cairo Citizen*, November 16, 1893.

23. "Wetaug News."

24. Owen Evers interview, 35–36.

25. For a more complete discussion of "hidden history" see Batinski, *Forgetting and the Forgotten*.

26. Butler, *Living in Cache Bottom*, 15, 32.

27. Butler, 59.

5. The Klan Goes to Church

1. "Klu Klux Clans Hold Meetings," *Pulaski Enterprise*, September 14, 1923.

2. "Grand Chain," *Cairo Evening Citizen*, October 1, 1923, and "Grand Chain," *Cairo Evening Citizen*, October 6, 1923.

3. "Crowd Attends K. K. K. Meeting at Grand Chain," *Cairo Evening Citizen*, September 14, 1923.

4. "Klu Klux Clans Hold Meetings."

5. Gordon, *Second Coming*, 96–97; Chalmers, *Hooded Americanism*,109.

6. Peterson, "Murder at Mer Rouge."

7. Pegram, *One Hundred Percent*, 174.

8. "Klan Presents Large Purse to Rev. Anderson," *Cairo Evening Citizen*, October 16, 1923.

9. Sutherland wrote at the beginning of his book, "Please accept my apologies for giving to the world the events recorded here, especially the things that were secrets between you and me. . . . There is no fiction in this book. Every incident recorded here is strictly true, and came under the personal observation of the author, but, as truth is stranger than fiction, I have taken the liberty of toning down the facts a little to give them the appearance of fiction."

10. Sutherland, *Then Cometh the Devil*, 38.

11. The Reverend Charles L. Dawdy was pastor of Washington Avenue Methodist Episcopal Church in Alton, Illinois. His brother was the Reverend Claude Carroll Dawdy of Brownstown, Illinois, also a Methodist minister.

12. "Thebes," *Cairo Evening Citizen*, February 27, 1924.

13. "Old Time Religion Preached at Mounds," *Cairo Evening Citizen*, November 7, 1923.

14. "Klan Gives Purse to Congregational Pastor," *Cairo Evening Citizen*, April 12, 1924.

15. Smith, *A History of Southern Illinois*, 719–721.

16. "Masked Kluxer Parades Barred in Williamson," *Cairo Evening Citizen*, August 29, 1924. Jesse Earl Ashbrook was originally from Mattoon, Coles County, Illinois, where he was part owner in a grain business.

17. In other parts of the state, the Klan was not received into the church. In Pana, Christian County, Illinois, the Reverend Frank Patton was dismissed from Assumption Christian Church in October 1923 because he gave several speeches or sermons on behalf of the Ku Klux Klan ("Minister Dismissed for Klan Activities," *Cairo Evening Citizen*, October 17, 1923).

18. "Ullin News," *Pulaski Enterprise*, April 25, 1924.

19. "Pulaski News," *Pulaski Enterprise*, June 27, 1924.

20. "Klan Gives Church Money for Preacher," *Cairo Evening Citizen*, August 20, 1924.

21. Pegram, *One Hundred Percent*, 28.

22. "Ullin News," *Cairo Evening Citizen*, October 19, 1923.

23. Gordon, *Second Coming*, 67.

24. "Large Crowd Attends Klan Meeting Here," *Cairo Evening Citizen*, January 25, 1924. The Reverend C. C. Crawford, pastor of the Christian church, is listed as one of the ministers who supported the Klan in an article that appeared in the *Christian Century*, October 25, 1923, page 1380. In 1925, Crawford was pastor of Fourth Christian Church, St. Louis, Missouri (*Polk-Gould 1925 St. Louis Directory*).

25. "Ullin News," *Cairo Evening Citizen*, February 8, 1924.

26. "Ullin News," *Pulaski Enterprise*, April 4, 1924.

27. "Klan Holds Initiation on Ullin Farm," *Cairo Evening Citizen*, June 12, 1924.

28. "Ullin News," *Pulaski Enterprise*, June 20, 1924.

29. Ayabe, "The Ku Klux Klan Movement in Williamson County, Illinois, 1923–1926," 28.

30. *Kloran*, 21.

31. *Kloran*, 21.

32. *Kloran*, 22.

33. *Kloran*, 23.

34. "Thousands Attend Thebes Klan Meet," *Cairo Evening Citizen*, June 16, 1924.

35. Dunphy, "A Brief History."

36. The parsonage in which the unmarried Rev. Charles D. McGehee lived with his parents, the Reverend J. S. and Mrs. McGehee, was at 6436 Vermont St., St. Louis, Missouri.

37. Letter from Bishop McMurry to Rev. Charles D. McGehee, March 8, 1923, William Fletcher McMurry Papers 1885–1934, folder 69.

38. "Methodist Bishop Puts Ban on Ku Klux Sermon," *Record*, March 15, 1923.

39. William Fletcher McMurry Papers, folder 67.

40. William Fletcher McMurry Papers, folder 69.

41. "Klan Preacher Is Suspended; Trial by Church Ordered," *Brooklyn Daily Eagle*, January 2, 1924.

42. "Legion Protests Klan Lecturer as a Chaplain," *National Catholic Welfare Conference News Sheet*, December 24, 1923.

43. "Rev. McGehee Doesn't Preach the Kind of a Sermon that Would Be Expected from a Man of His Name," *Fiery Cross* 2, no. 21, April 27, 1923.

44. "Ministers Support the Klan," *Christian Century*, October 25, 1923. He spoke on the "ideals of klanism," called for the closing of Ellis Island, and oversaw the initiation of 250 klansmen in Murphysboro in October 1923 (*Murphysboro Daily Independent*, October 10, 1923; October 16, 1923).

45. "Church Body Upholds Ouster of McGehee," *St. Louis Daily Post-Dispatch*, December 7, 1923.

46. William Fletcher McMurry Papers, folder 67.

47. William Fletcher McMurry Papers, folder 71, trial transcript page 61; Jackson, *Ku Klux Klan*, 163.

48. "Klan," *Cairo Evening Citizen*, July 5, 1924. According to the Klan, 2,000 people paid to park and about 1,100 automobiles were counted by a Cairo newspaper representative.

49. "Thousands Spent Fourth in Cairo," *Carbondale Daily Free Press*, July 5, 1924.

50. Beadles, *Stained with Blood*, 73–80.

51. "Chicago Negress to Speak Here," *Cairo Evening Citizen*, March 17, 1924.

52. The Cairo Civic City League, "an organization of colored citizens" was presided over by W. A. Singleton. That organization was also active in bringing prominent

African American speakers to Cairo during this era (*Cairo Evening Citizen*, February 15, 1924).

53. "Ministers to Tell About Williamson County," *Cairo Evening Citizen*, March 17, 1924.

54. "Ministers to Tell."

55. "County Ministerial Association Formed," *Pulaski Enterprise*, January 25, 1924; "Wrong Impression Is Created," *Pulaski Enterprise*, February 8, 1924. The Reverend Roy N. Kean claimed that the members of the Pulaski County Ministerial Alliance were not drawing a color line. The first vice president of the organization was the Reverend C. L. Phifer of Ullin, who was associated with the Ku Klux Klan.

56. "Pastor Assails Politicians in Williamson County," *Cairo Evening Citizen*, March 19, 1924.

57. "Mounds News," *Cairo Evening Citizen*, May 2, 1924.

58. "Klan Defies City Council; to Meet," *Cairo Evening Citizen*, May 23, 1924.

59. "Harrisburg," *Pulaski Enterprise*, May 9, 1924.

60. "Harrisburg Mob Failed to Get Negro," *Cairo Evening Citizen*, May 5, 1924.

61. "Klan Trouble in Negro Church Goes to Court," *Cairo Evening Citizen*, August 23, 1924.

62. Pegram, *One Hundred Percent*, 24–25.

63. "Negro Preacher Fined for Assault," *Cairo Evening Citizen*, August 25, 1924.

64. "Seek Negro Who Murdered a Policeman," *Cairo Evening Citizen*, January 2, 1923.

65. "Negro Admits to Eight Deaths, Other Crimes," *Cairo Evening Citizen*, February 9, 1923.

66. "One Killed, Seven Hurt, as Negro Cuts," *Cairo Evening Citizen*, February 15, 1923.

67. "Crippled White Man Attacked by Negro," *Pulaski Enterprise*, October 5, 1923.

68. "Negro Sent Up 21 Years for Murder," *Cairo Evening Citizen*, October 20, 1923.

69. "Negress Denies Giving Poison to Children," *Cairo Evening Citizen*, November 14, 1923.

70. "Negro Shoots Youth Then Attacks Girl," *Cairo Evening Citizen*, December 26, 1923.

71. "Negro Held for Assault to Kill," *Cairo Evening Citizen*, March 27, 1924.

72. "Olmsted Boy Is Killed by Negro," *Pulaski Enterprise*, October 17, 1924.

73. "Escaped Negro Murderer Caught Near Sandusky," *Pulaski Enterprise*, December 14, 1924.

74. "Nation Gets the Boot in Mound City," *Pulaski Enterprise*, February 20, 1925.

75. Pegram, *One Hundred Percent*, 54.

76. "Large Congregation Hears Rabbi Sadler's Farewell," *Cairo Bulletin*, May 18, 1908.

77. Shevitz, *Jewish Communities*, 121.

6. The Elco Trouble

1. "Ullin News," *Pulaski Enterprise*, Friday, January 11, 1924.

2. "Elco Is Quiet after Shooting There Tuesday," *Cairo Evening Citizen*, January 10, 1924.

3. "Negroes and Whites Battle at Cairo," *Carbondale Daily Free Press*, January 11, 1924.

4. "Negro Shot in Battle near Elco," *Cairo Evening Citizen*, January 9, 1924.

5. The 1920 census identifies two physicians living in Tamms, Illinois, Dr. James Knox Rosson, 29, and Dr. Alfred Rowe Penniman, 59. There were no physicians in Elco in 1920 or 1930. Two physicians, Dr. John Brown Mathis and Dr. Luther F. Robinson, lived in nearby Ullin in 1920 and 1930.

6. "Elco Negro Is out of Hospital," *Cairo Evening Citizen*, January 28, 1924.

7. "Negroes and Whites Battle at Cairo," *Carbondale Daily Free Press*, January 11, 1924.

8. "Announcements," *Cairo Bulletin*, September 10, 1918.

9. Cotton could be planted in southern Illinois after the last frost, typically in mid-May (Evans, Hackleman, and Bauer, "Cotton Growing in Illinois," 6).

10. Perrin, *A History of Alexander*, 436.

11. *Official Records of the War*, 521.

12. "Large Cotton Field," *Cairo Daily Times*, October 8, 1865, quoting *Illinois State Journal*.

13. "An Outrageous Procedure," *Cairo Daily Times*, October 10, 1865.

14. "Personal," *Cairo Daily Times*, October 26, 1865.

15. "To the Land of Cotton," *Cairo Bulletin*, September 29, 1905.

16. "Waitin' on de Levee Foh Dat Lee Line Whistle," *Cairo Bulletin*, September 11, 1913; "300 Negroes Leave for the Cotton Fields," *Cairo Bulletin*, September 20, 1913.

17. "Negroes Threatened: Unsigned Letters Warn Colored Population of Hickman, Ky., to Leave," *Cairo Bulletin*, May 20, 1908.

18. "Hickman, Ky., District Wants 300 Cotton Pickers as Soon as Possible," *Cairo Bulletin*, October 10, 1914.

19. "KuKlux in Ballard Co.—Farmer Warned Not to Employ Illinois Negroes," *Cairo Bulletin*, April 3, 1904.

20. "Barlow, Ky.," *Cairo Bulletin*, July 20, 1904.

21. "Dynamite at La Center," *Cairo Bulletin*, August 5, 1904.

22. "Race War Has Come to an End—Negroes Leave and Rioters Are Placed behind Bars," *Cairo Bulletin*, September 16, 1905.

23. "Woman Tells of Her Escape—Mrs. Margaret DeLaney's Account of Lumber Camp Battle," *Cairo Bulletin*, September 18, 1905. Seven members of the mob were arrested and placed in jail under a $500 bond. They were Lon Hughes, Wood Hughes, Jesse Wilson, Charles Wilson, G. D. Campbell, Will Dunn, and J. A. McHood.

24. This was likely Dr. Lee Thomas Fox, a physician in Sumner, Tallahatchie County, Mississippi. In addition to being a doctor, he grew up on a farm and owned his own farm in Yazoo City, Mississippi. His son, William A. Fox, was a cotton buyer, according to his 1921 passport application.

25. "Negro Farm Labor," *Jonesboro Gazette*, February 8, 1924; "Cotton Boom to Cairo," *Cairo Evening Citizen*, February 4, 1924. Cairo had two cotton seed oil mills before 1923, but the cotton was grown south of the Ohio River.

26. "Why Not Rent Some of Land to Cotton Growers?," *Pulaski Enterprise*, February 2, 1923.

27. *Cairo Evening Citizen*, January 23, 1924; "$2,000,000 Cotton Crop in Two Counties," *Cairo Evening Citizen*, January 24, 1924.

28. "Local Cotton Growers Discuss Co-Operative Marketing," *Pulaski Enterprise*, July 4, 1924.

29. By December 1924, the Smallen Gin had turned 339 bales of cotton, and the Murphy Gin had 272 bales ("Cotton Gins Have Ginned over 600 Bales," *Pulaski Enterprise*, December 14, 1924). G. J. Murphy bought a new cotton gin in Memphis, Tennessee, and erected it in the ice plant at Mound City during the summer of 1924 ("Murphy Buys Cotton Gin in the South," *Pulaski Enterprise*, June 27, 1924). Thomas O. Smallen of Vanndale, Arkansas, also installed a gin in the Williamson & Kuny warehouse at Mound City during the summer of 1924 ("Mound City Will Have Two Cotton Gins," *Pulaski Enterprise*, July 18, 1924).

30. "Local News," *Jonesboro Gazette*, October 5, 1923.

31. "Cotton Gin," *Jonesboro Gazette*, August 15, 1924. If the report is accurate, this was a large investment in cotton production. Adjusted for inflation, $18,000 in 1924 is the equivalent of about $315,000 in 2023.

32. "Reward," *Jonesboro Gazette*, February 8, 1924. The name was pronounced "Doo Boys," as in W. E. B. DuBois, instead of "Doob Wah."

33. "One at Anna," *Cairo Bulletin*, November 15, 1909.

34. "Offers $1,000 Reward for Dynamiters," *Cairo Evening Citizen*, November 21, 1910.

35. "Negroes and Cotton," *Jonesboro Gazette*, February 29, 1924, quoting *Cairo Bulletin*. Darrell James was 37 years old in 1924, and he and his wife, Mary Rachel (Newell) James, lived in Elco.

36. "Negroes and Cotton."

37. "Blast Damages Cotton Picker's House at Elco," *Cairo Evening Citizen*, January 30, 1924.

38. "Cauble Candidate for Sheriff," *Cairo Bulletin*, April 13, 1914.

39. Dora Beasley identified the man whose child she had carried and the doctor who performed the abortion. Dr. Robinson was charged with malpractice and performing the procedure, which was illegal at the time. He claimed Dora came to his office under an assumed name seeking medical care after she had attempted an abortion on herself. Dora's deathbed confession was ruled inadmissible in court, and the case against Dr. Robinson was dismissed November 21, 1904.

40. "An Elco Citizen Is Under Arrest—Israel Cauble Charged with Knocking Down a Well Known Woman," *Cairo Bulletin*, August 31, 1906.

41. "Israel Cauble for Assault," *Cairo Bulletin*, September 4, 1906. Fourteen years later, Deputy William White's son married the daughter of Israel Cauble.

42. "Offer Reward for Terrorists Around Elco," *Cairo Evening Citizen*, March 4, 1924.

43. "Offer Reward."

44. "Maj. Greaney Is Ordered to Elco District," *Cairo Evening Citizen*, March 5, 1924.

45. "No Indictments Yet Returned in Elco Jury Quiz," *Cairo Evening Citizen*, March 12, 1924.

46. "Cauble Tells Grand Jury of Elco Trouble," *Cairo Evening Citizen*, March 13, 1924.

47. "Expect Report of Jury Monday," *Cairo Evening Citizen*, March 15, 1924.

48. "9 Indictments Are Returned by Elco Jury," *Cairo Evening Citizen*, March 17, 1924.

49. Alexander Criminal Record Book 30, 262.

50. "Two Deputy Sheriffs in Elco Trouble," *Cairo Evening Citizen*, March 18, 1924.

51. "All but One of Elco Men Are Arrested," *Cairo Evening Citizen*, March 20, 1924. Ed Bryden and George W. Miller were commissioned deputies to replace the Brown brothers.

52. "One Man Still Wanted in Elco Racial Trouble," *Cairo Evening Citizen*, March 21, 1924.

53. Alexander Criminal Record Book 30, 262–263.

54. Alexander Criminal Record Book 30, 263.

55. "All Elco Men out on Bond," *Cairo Evening Citizen*, March 22, 1924.

56. "Other Inmates Prevent Break from County Jail," *Cairo Evening Citizen*, March 21, 1924.

57. "All Elco Men out"; Alexander Criminal Record Book 30, 264.

58. Alexander Criminal Record Book 30, 264.

59. "All but One of Elco Men."

60. "One Man Still Wanted in Elco Racial Trouble," *Cairo Evening Citizen*, March 21, 1924.

61. "All but One of Elco Men."

62. Alexander Criminal Record Book 30, 267.

63. "Butler Denies Motion to Kill Elco Charges," *Cairo Evening Citizen*, May 17, 1924.

64. Alexander Criminal Record Book 30, 271.

65. "Assault Charge against Deputy Sheriffs Dropped," *Cairo Evening Citizen*, January 8, 1925; Alexander Criminal Record Book 30, 293; "Postpone Trial of Elco Men in Race Disorder," *Cairo Evening Citizen*, May 22, 1924.

66. "Assault Charges against Deputy Sheriffs Dropped."

67. Years later, Burleigh Brown claimed that a still had been planted in his coal house by Sheriff Roche. Brown told a Cairo law enforcement officer, "I'd like to have my place raided so I could plead guilty to possession and tell where that still had come from" ("Convict Tells of Protection Given Him Here," *Cairo Evening Citizen and Cairo Bulletin*, December 11, 1928).

68. There were 86 "Negroes" listed in the census of Tamms, all living south of the gravel pit switch, in 1930.

7. For Twenty-Six Pennies

1. Among the neighbors were Bob Endicott, Lou Endicott, Elmer Koonce, Earl Helman, Bill Bour, and Steve Lampley.

2. "Klansman's Prayer Probably Prevents Lynching at Mounds," *Cairo Evening Citizen*, July 22, 1924.

3. "Another Confession to Murder Is Obtained," *Cairo Bulletin*, July 28, 1924.

4. "Another Confession to Murder."

5. There was also a 31-year-old son, Glenn Alvin Wilson, who had returned home in 1920 after serving five years in Mexico during the Border Campaign and later through World War I. He had left on a trip to South America and had arrived at New Orleans 10 days earlier, on July 11, and it is unlikely that he had returned to southern Illinois by the night of his sister's murder since he was not mentioned in newspaper accounts of the incident.

6. "Villa Ridge Girl Murdered by Unknown Negro Robbers," *Pulaski Enterprise*, July 25, 1924.

7. "Whole Tragedy Revolved over Just 26 Cents," *Cairo Evening Citizen*, August 9, 1924.

8. "Negroes Murder Girl in Attempted Hold-Up," *Cairo Bulletin*, July 22, 1924.

9. Bloodhounds had been utilized successfully to track or trail missing persons and fugitives since the Middle Ages in Europe, but in the antebellum South they were mostly used to capture fugitives fleeing slavery. Although the days of slave patrols had ended more than 60 years earlier, the past was not so distant that memories of slave hounds running down fugitives had completely disappeared. In 1909 bloodhounds were used to hunt down Will "Froggie" James, the alleged murderer and rapist of Anna Pelley in Cairo, and had been used to track other suspected criminals.

10. "Lynchers' Little Mistakes," *St. Louis Post Dispatch*, July 24, 1924.

11. "Wilson Girl Tragedy Kills Seymour Welch," *Pulaski Enterprise*, July 25, 1924.

8. The Lynch Mob and the Klansman's Prayer

1. "Negro Slayers Escape Mob Bent on Lynching, Chase Murders of White Girl for Miles," *Carbondale Daily Free Press*, July 22, 1924.

2. Dray, *At the Hands of Persons Unknown*, ix.

3. Berg, *Popular Justice*, 92.

4. "Lynchings by Year and Race."

5. Before 1900, there were 15 lynchings or attempted lynchings documented in Alexander and Pulaski Counties; eight were Black men and seven were White men.

6. "Illinois Lynching," *Los Angeles Herald*, April 27, 1903. The coroner's jury met on April 27, 1903, and stated that Johnson was "an unknown negro man" and that he was lynched by "parties unknown" (Alexander County Coroner's Record, page 91). See also "Lynch Negro; Raid Camp," *Chicago Tribune*, Monday, April 27, 1903.

7. "Thebes Lynchers," *Cairo Evening Citizen*, December 28, 1903; "Circuit Court Meets," *Cairo Bulletin*, February 9, 1904. See also "Thebes Lynching Case," *Cairo Evening Citizen*, January 18, 1904; "To Try Two Big Murder Cases," *Cairo Evening Citizen*, February 5, 1904; "Johnson Was Released," *Cairo Evening Citizen*, February 18, 1904; "Jury Did Not Agree," *Cairo Evening Citizen*, October 24, 1903; "Four Prisoners Effect Escape," *Cairo Bulletin*, April 10, 1904; "In Circuit Court Hickson Murder Case Nollied and Defendant Released from Jail," *Cairo Evening Citizen*, May 11, 1904.

8. "Six Months in Jail," *Cairo Evening Citizen*, July 29, 1903. Harry Pettit and Ed Laish were also tried for participation in the riot but were found not guilty ("Thebes Rioting Case," *Cairo Evening Citizen*, July 28, 1903).

9. "Released Thebes Men," *Cairo Evening Citizen*, December 29, 1903. Evidence showed that Pettit had actually tried to stop the lynching and Laish was judged to be mentally irresponsible ("Six Months in Jail," *Cairo Evening Citizen*, July 29, 1903). Alexander County Criminal Record Book, People v. Fred Kenner, Henry Metcalf, and William Slauson, case No. 2360.

10. "Identification Was Complete," *Cairo Bulletin*, July 21, 1904.

11. "Sympathizers Fined," *Cairo Bulletin*, July 3, 1904.

12. "Verdict Is Rendered," *Cairo Bulletin*, July 25, 1904. Mason applied for a pardon on July 14, 1908 ("Petition for Pardon," *Cairo Bulletin*, June 13, 1908).

13. "Negro Is in Jail," *Cairo Bulletin*, July 25, 1905.

14. "Negro Assaulted Young White Girl," *Cairo Bulletin*, July 24, 1905.

15. "Conflicting Tales of Fight," *Cairo Bulletin*, September 19, 1905; "Death of W. O. Bruce," *Cairo Evening Citizen*, September 19, 1905.

16. "Mob Formed at Mounds Tried to Lynch Negro," *Cairo Bulletin*, July 31, 1906. Samuel Lee McDonald was born June 14, 1887, in Huntingdon, Carroll County, Tennessee, the son of Alexander McDonald and Hattie Woodson, according to his delayed birth certificate. The World War I draft registration for Homer Travis filed from the Southern Illinois Penitentiary at Menard stated he was born September 19, 1887, in Paris, Illinois.

17. "Man Hunt on in Pulaski County—Negro Slays White Man and Pitched Battle Follows," *Cairo Bulletin*, July 30, 1906; "Negro Slayer of Homer Harris at Large," *Cairo Bulletin*, August 1, 1906.

18. Homer Travis was apprehended in Tennessee by Lee Walton, "a colored detective of Ullin," and returned to Pulaski County ("Honor to Whom It Is Due," *Cairo Bulletin*, September 19, 1906). Travis pleaded guilty and was sentenced to 20 years in the Southern Illinois Penitentiary at Chester for murder. McDonald pleaded guilty to manslaughter and was sent to the state reformatory ("Ullin Murderers Are Sentenced," *Cairo Evening Citizen*, January 15, 1907). McDonald was released after a few years and married Hattie McCain on November 25, 1909, in Pulaski County.

19. Beadles, *Stained with Blood*, 36–48.

20. Beadles, 41–42.

21. Beadles, 49–54.

22. Beadles, 112–135.

23. "Posse Kills Negro at Tamms," *Cairo Evening Citizen*, September 12, 1913.

24. "Negroes Amuck; One Lynched," *Chicago Daily Tribune*, September 13, 1913.

25. His name was called Calvin Wisdom in "A Brutal Murder," *Pulaski Enterprise*, June 20, 1919. He was called Taylor Wisdom in the *Pulaski Enterprise*, August 1, 1919. He was called Caylour Wisdom in the *Mounds News*, August 7, 1919, and in the Pulaski County court record. The name of his wife was not recorded in the newspaper accounts or court records, and a coroner's record could not be located. She did not have a death certificate filed in Pulaski County. See also "Grand Chain Mob Lynches Wife Murderer," *Mounds News*, June 20, 1919.

26. Pulaski Circuit Court Book 14, 537. The original case file No. 1133 was missing or misfiled and could not be located at the courthouse.

27. "Lynching of Negro Prisoners Threatened," *Cairo Bulletin*, July 23, 1924. "Villa Ridge Girl Murdered by Unknown Negro Robbers," *Pulaski Enterprise*, July 25, 1924; "Negro Slayers Escape."
28. "Lynching of Negro Prisoners Threatened."
29. Pegram, *One Hundred Percent*, 60.
30. "Villa Ridge Girl Murdered."
31. "Villa Ridge Girl Murdered."
32. "Reward Offered for Murderers of Daisy Wilson," *Cairo Bulletin*, July 26, 1924.

9. Railroad Detectives and the National Guard

1. "May Be Wrong Two Negroes," *Carbondale Daily Free Press*, July 23, 1924.
2. "May Be Wrong."
3. "Lynching of Negro Prisoners Threatened," *Cairo Bulletin* added West Frankfort cars at the courthouse (July 23, 1924).
4. "Negro Suspects Taken Away," *Cairo Evening Citizen*, July 23, 1924; "Villa Ridge Girl Murdered by Unknown Negro Robbers," *Pulaski Enterprise*, July 25, 1924.
5. "Villa Ridge Girl Murdered."
6. "Lynching of Negro Prisoners Threatened"; "Murder at Villa Ridge," *Jonesboro Gazette*, July 25, 1924.
7. "Lynching of Negro Prisoners Threatened."
8. Mound City once had a company of Illinois National Guardsmen, but they were disbanded in June 1904 and replaced with Company K, stationed in Cairo.
9. "Mound City Quiet after Mob Threat," *Cairo Evening Citizen*, July 23, 1924.
10. "How St. Louis Man Saw Demonstration at Mound City Jail," *Cairo Bulletin*, July 24, 1924.
11. "How St. Louis Man Saw Demonstration."
12. "May Offer Rewards for Slayers," *Cairo Evening Citizen*, July 24, 1924.
13. "Notice $200 Reward," *Pulaski Enterprise*, July 25, 1924.
14. "How St. Louis Man Saw Demonstration."
15. "Negro Suspects Taken Away."
16. "Negro Suspects Taken away but Mob Is Rampant," *Cairo Evening Citizen*, July 23, 1924.
17. "Lynching of Negro Prisoners Threatened."
18. "Villa Ridge Girl Murdered."
19. "Villa Ridge Girl Murdered."
20. "May Be Wrong Two Negroes."
21. "Negroes Enter Plea of Guilty for Girl Slaying," *Carbondale Free Press*, July 30, 1924.

22. "Description Answers One of Murderer," *Cairo Evening Citizen*, July 25, 1924.

23. "Trail Is Found of Negro Slayers in City," *Carbondale Daily Free Press*, July 24, 1924; *Cairo Bulletin*, July 26, 1924.

24. "Order Arrest of Carbondale Negro as Slayer of Girl," *Carbondale Daily Free Press*, July 25, 1924.

25. "Cairo Negro Sentenced to Hang for Slaying Miss Daisy Wilson," *Pulaski Enterprise*, August 1, 1924.

26. "Quick Justice for Slayers," *Carbondale Daily Free Press*, July 28, 1924. Julia (Bledsoe) Bryant, the sister of Hess Conner's mother, was born January 7, 1880, in Trenton, Gibson County, Tennessee, and died April 9, 1941, in Cairo, Illinois, according to her death certificate.

27. "Implicates Partner already under Arrest in Villa Ridge Case," *Cairo Evening Citizen*, July 26, 1924.

28. D. Holder is likely William Delevan Holder, who was a railroad employee in Jackson County, Illinois.

29. "Doubt Now that Negro Slayers Were Ever Here," *Carbondale Daily Free Press*, July 26, 1924; "Quick Justice for Slayer."

30. "Investigation Now Underway for Mob Action," *Cairo Evening Citizen*, July 29, 1924. The grand jury comprised William Spaulding, Villa Ridge; John Newell, Ernest Williams, and E. C. Droge, Mounds; Oliver Wallace, and Newt Shoffner, Pulaski; Louis Needham and Clarence Kelly, Ullin; E. C. West, Wetaug; Rev. W. H. Cole, Rev. L. A. Clark, and B. Hutcheson, Mound City; Walter Schnaare, America; Sim Taylor, Olmsted; and Ralph Esque, Jack Brannan, and George Bashears, of Grand Chain ("Negro Slayers Indicted on First Degree Murder," *Carbondale Daily Free Press*, July 29, 1924, 1).

31. Milton Dee Brelsford, from Mayfield, Kentucky, married Cornelia Lyerly on November 17, 1897, in Pulaski County, Illinois.

32. "Indictments Expected by Jury at Once," *Cairo Evening Citizen*, Monday, July 28, 1924.

33. "Villa Ridge Girl Murdered."

34. This seems to have been typical, as when Lee Walton, "a colored detective of Ullin," tracked Homer Travis, the alleged murderer of Homer Harris, to Tennessee, apprehended him, and returned him to Pulaski County, a Cairo newspaper initially credited Sheriff Gaunt with the arrest. The newspaper stated, "Sheriff Gaunt seems to have been untiring in his determination to capture him [Travis] and deserves credit for his success in running the man down" ("Negro Who Killed Mound City Man at Ullin Run Down in Tennessee and Landed in Jail," *Cairo Bulletin*, September 15, 1906).

35. "Lynchers' Little Mistakes," *Cairo Bulletin*, July 25, 1924.

36. "Villa Ridge Girl Murdered."

10. The Trial of Hale and Conner

1. "Cairo Negro Sentenced to Hang for Slaying Miss Daisy Wilson," *Pulaski Enterprise*, August 1, 1924.

2. "Given Chance by Court to Change Pleas," *Cairo Evening Citizen*, July 30, 1924; Pulaski County Circuit Court Book 21, 206.

3. Pulaski Circuit Court Book 21, 208.

4. Pulaski Circuit Court Book 21, 210.

5. "Conners to Hang Next Friday at Court House in This City," *Pulaski Enterprise*, October 10, 1924.

6. Pulaski Circuit Court Book 21, 210.

7. "Many Angles to Case Which Stirred County," *Cairo Evening Citizen*, January 16, 1925.

8. "Cairo Negro Sentenced to Hang for Slaying Miss Daisy Wilson"; Pulaski Circuit Court Book 21, 210.

9. "Slayer Given Death Penalty by Hartwell; Hale to Penitentiary," *Cairo Evening Citizen*, July 31, 1924.

10. "Conners to Hang Next Friday at Court House in This City," *Pulaski Enterprise*, October 10, 1924.

11. All of Hess Conner's siblings were born in Gibson County, Tennessee, and included: Mattie Lee Wade (1896–1934), Lillie M. Conner (1899–), Ossie May Bell (1903–), Willie T. Conner (1907–1941), and Lessie B. Conner (1909–). His half-siblings were Leroy Thery Nash (1910–1981), Clara Jones Sevier Dance (1912–1988), and Adeline Nash (1913–1917).

12. "Begin Building Stockade for Hess Conner," *Cairo Evening Citizen*, October 13, 1924. The scaffold had been built in 1915 for the execution of Joseph De-Berry, a Black man accused of murdering a White woman ("The Danger of a Bad Precedent in Public Execution," *Los Angeles Herald*, October 30, 1915). It was used five times before it was borrowed by Pulaski County. A sixth man had been sentenced to hang from it but received a last-hour commutation to life in prison ("Sheriff Tears Down Conners Scaffold," *Pulaski Enterprise*, October 31, 1924).

13. "Gallows from This County to Hang Negro," *Carbondale Daily Free Press*, October 14, 1924.

14. "Hess Conners Hanged at Mound City Yesterday," *Cairo Bulletin*, January 17, 1925. Lela A. (Bledsoe) Conner Nash was born December 24, 1878, in Gibson County, Tennessee, the daughter of Mit Bledsoe and Nancy Sharp, and married Paul Conner on November 1, 1894, in Gibson County. After Paul died, she married James A. "Jim" Nash on December 12, 1909, in Gibson County. At the time of her son's arrest, she was still living on Meridian Highway in Gibson County.

15. "Condemned Negro Is Reprieved," *Pulaski Enterprise*, October 17, 1924.

16. "Seek 90 Day Reprieve for Hess Conner," *Cairo Evening Citizen*, October 14, 1924.

17. "Little Chance for Conner to Escape Noose," *Cairo Evening Citizen*, October 11, 1924.

18. "Reprieved Until January 16," *Cairo Evening Citizen*, October 15, 1924.

19. "Conners to Hang, Unless Committee Reports Him Insane," *Pulaski Enterprise*, January 9, 1925.

20. "Conners Again Hears Hammers on His Scaffold," *Cairo Evening Citizen*, January 12, 1925.

21. "Mob Member Given 30 Days in Jail," *Cairo Evening Citizen*, January 15, 1925.

22. "Hess Conners' Health Failing in Last Hours," *Cairo Evening Citizen*, January 14, 1925.

23. "Paid Penalty on Gallows," *Cairo Evening Citizen*, February 17, 1905.

24. "Twentieth Anniversary of the Hanging of Eli Bugg Feb. 17th in This City," *Pulaski Enterprise*, February 13, 1925; "Cairo Negro Sentenced to Hang for Slaying Miss Daisy Wilson."

25. "Eli Bugg Hanged!!," *Pulaski Enterprise*, February 17, 1905.

26. The Reverend J. M. Sutherland referred to Eli Bugg as "Bill Bugg, the Black Snake" in his 1907 book *Then Cometh the Devil* (Butler, IN: Luther H. Higley). In his account, the death of Bugg was a lynching in which the lynchers voted by ballot whether to murder Bugg (268–271).

27. "Jury Says Eli Bugg Must Hang," *Cairo Evening Citizen*, September 19, 1904, quoting the *Mound City Sun*.

28. "Paid Penalty on the Gallows," *Cairo Evening Citizen*, February 17, 1905.

29. "Eli Bugg Hanged!!"

30. Copies of the photographs could not be located by the authors.

31. "Facing Eternity Tomorrow Hess Conners Laughed and Kidded Friends Yesterday," *Cairo Bulletin*, January 15, 1925.

32. "Hess Conners Hanged at Mound City."

33. "Hess Conners Hanged at Mound City."

34. "Hess Conners Hanged at Mound City." It is not clear which brother this was. At the time he had three: Willie T. Conner, 18; Lessie B. Conner, 16; and Leroy T. Nash, 14.

35. "Sheriff Hudson in Fine Condition Following Hanging," *Pulaski Enterprise*, January 23, 1925.

36. "Sheriff Hudson in Fine Condition."

37. "Sheriff Hudson in Fine Condition."

38. "Hess Conners Hanged at Mound City."

39. "Hess Conners Dies on Gallows This Morning," *Pulaski Enterprise*, January 17, 1925.

40. "Hess Conners Hanged at Mound City."

41. "Hess Conners Dies on Gallows."

42. The *Cairo Bulletin* stated that Wilson viewed the hanging from a window in the courthouse ("Hess Conners Hanged at Mound City").

43. "Hess Conners Dies Game on Gallows," *Cairo Evening Citizen*, January 16, 1925.

44. The coroner's jury consisted of Chief of Police Harry Gilmore; James Davidge, of Cairo; Otto Betts, of Mound City; Ed Gore, of Olmsted; Ollis Victor, of Grand Chain; Ed Beiswingert, of Mounds; S. H. Needham, of Ullin; and E. C. Fletcher.

45. "Hess Conners Hanged at Mound City."

46. "Hess Conners Hanged at Mound City."

47. "Hess Conners Hanged at Mound City."

48. Moyers, *Brief History of Pulaski County, 1843–1943*, 36.

49. "Sheriff Hudson in Fine Condition."

50. Pfeifer, *Rough Justice*, 131.

11. Lynch Mob Indictments and Trial

1. The grand jury was composed of Will Spaulding, Mounds, foreman; John Newell, Mounds; Ernest Williams, Mounds; E. C. Droge, Mounds; Oliver Wallace, Pulaski; Newt Shoffner, Pulaski; Louis Needham, Ullin; Clarence Kelly, Ullin; E. C. West, Wetaug; Rev. W. H. Cole, Mound City; Rev. L. A. Clark, Mound City; B. Hutcheson, Mound City; Walter Schnaare, America; Sim Taylor, Olmsted; Ralph Escue, Grand Chain; Jack Brannon, Grand Chain; and George Beshears, Grand Chain.

2. "Authorities Afraid Mob Made Escape of Real Culprits Easy," *Cairo Evening Citizen*, July 24, 1924; "To Indict Mob Leaders," *Carbondale Free Daily Press*, July 24, 1924.

3. The indictment listed the following witnesses: Charles Walbridge Sr., B. L. Hendrix, E. A. Beiswingert, Charles Walbridge Jr., Walter W. White, Paul Salmon, J. M. Bonner, Charles Vanderpool, Thomas B. Aldrich, Forrest Moreland, Ollie C. Walker, W. C. Perks, I. J. Hudson, and Logan Davis (Illinois State Archives).

4. "Indict 9 Mob Heads," *Cairo Evening Citizen*, July 31, 1924.

5. Pulaski County Circuit Court Book 21, 213. The case file was 1267, but the record was missing or misfiled and could not be located in the courthouse basement.

6. People v. Winters.

7. *Winters.*

8. *Winters.*

9. "Only Two Yet Located on Mob Charges," *Cairo Evening Citizen*, August 4, 1924. The circuit court record listed their names as Mack Morris and John Bradbury.

10. "7 Charged with Leading Mob Still at Large," *Daily Free Press*, August 4 1924.

11. "No Further Arrests in Mound City Mob," *Cairo Evening Citizen*, August 5, 1924. Winters was later arrested by Sheriff Hudson on August 16, 1924 ("Sheriff Arrests Winters for Mob Participation," *Pulaski Enterprise*, August 22, 1924).

12. "The Mob Leaders Found by Sheriff," *Pulaski Enterprise*, August 8, 1924.

13. "Pulaski County Law Abiding," *Cairo Bulletin*, July 25, 1924.

14. "Cairo Negro Confesses Girls Murder," *Cairo Evening Citizen*, July 28, 1924.

15. "Quick Justice," *Cairo Bulletin*, August 1, 1924.

16. "Continue Cases of Mob Leaders," *Cairo Evening Citizen*, August 16, 1924.

17. "Another Mob Leader Held in Kentucky," *Cairo Evening Citizen*, September 6, 1924.

18. Secretary of State. The requisition files from 1923 to 1925, the governor's journal, and miscellaneous orders at the Kentucky State Archives were also searched, but no record of the denial of the requisition was located there.

19. "Will Not Extradite Alleged Mob Leader," *Decatur Herald*, September 28, 1924.

20. "Riot Trials Are Set Next Week in Mound City," *Cairo Evening Citizen*, October 23, 1924.

21. "Riot Trials Are Set."

22. "Criminal Docket Cut Down by Session This Week," *Pulaski Enterprise*, January 16, 1925.

23. "Hess Conners Hanged at Mound City Yesterday," *Cairo Bulletin*, January 17, 1925.

24. Pulaski Circuit Court Book 21, 233.

25. "Carmi Man in Final Test of Gallows," *Cairo Evening Citizen*, January 15, 1925; Pulaski Circuit Court Book 21, 248.

26. Pulaski Circuit Court Book 21, 248.

27. Butler, *Living in Cache Bottom*, 135.

28. *Lynching in America*, 46.

29. *Lynching in America*, 46.

30. Berg, *Popular Justice*, 262.

12. The Second Klan Fades from Memory

1. "35,000 in Klan Garb Parade in Washington," *Sun*, August 9, 1925.

2. "Burning Cross 80 Feet High Ends Gathering," *Cairo Evening Citizen*, August 10, 1925.

3. Gordon, *Second Coming*, 114.

4. "As He Was," *Cairo Evening Citizen*, February 13, 1924.

5. Gordon, *Second Coming*, 17–18.

6. Pegram, *One Hundred Percent*, 206.

7. "Church Body Upholds Ouster of McGehee," *St. Louis Daily Post-Dispatch*, December 17, 1923.

8. "St. Louis Legion Opposes Kluxers," *Indianapolis Times*, December 18, 1923.

9. "Klan Pastor to Face Trial by Methodists," *Evening Star*, January 2, 1924.

10. Ayabe, "Ku Klux Klan," 167.

11. Angle, *Bloody Williamson*, 161.

12. Angle, 161.

13. Galligan, *In Bloody Williamson*, 20; Chalmers, *Hooded Americanism*, 188.

14. Galligan, 28; "Company K Leaves for Williamson," *Cairo Evening Citizen*, February 9, 1924; Ayabe, "Ku Klux Klan," 38.

15. "Young Deposed as Head of South Illinois Klan," *Cairo Evening Citizen*, July 16, 1924.

16. Pegram, *One Hundred Percent*, 185–187.

17. Pegram, 25.

18. Chalmers, *Hooded Americanism*, 40.

19. U.S. Census, Georgia.

20. Ayabe, "Ku Klux Klan," 251–252.

21. Gordon, *Second Coming*, 191.

22. "Ku Klux Klan in Illinois."

23. In 1942 he worked for the Illinois Treasury Department as a state investigator and lived in the Carlton Hotel in Danville. He died June 4, 1977, in Lourdes Hospital, Paducah, Kentucky (*Metropolis Planet*, June 9, 1977).

24. "Rev. W. P. Anderson Gives Farewell Sermon," *Cairo Evening Citizen*, November 3, 1924.

25. The Reverend William Paul Anderson was born January 27, 1888, and died October 20, 1958, in Rochelle, Texas, where he was buried.

26. Butler, *Living in Cache Bottom*, 134.

27. Butler, 135.

28. Pegram, *One Hundred Percent*, 181.

29. "Sheriff Nabs White Woman and Negro Man in Bed Here," *Pulaski Enterprise*, March 6, 1925.

30. No record of the case could be found in 1925 circuit court books in Pulaski County.

Newspapers

Broad Ax (Chicago)
Brooklyn (NY) *Daily Eagle*
Cairo (IL) *Argus and Mound City Journal*
Cairo (IL) *Bulletin*
Cairo (IL) *Citizen*
Cairo (IL) *Daily Democrat*
Cairo (IL) *Evening Citizen*
Cairo (IL) *Evening Citizen and Cairo Bulletin*
Cairo (IL) *Evening Times*
Carbondale (IL) *Daily Free Press*
Chicago Daily Tribune
Christian Century (Chicago)
Daily Argus (Rock Island, IL)
Daily Freeman (Waukesha, WI)
Daily Journal and Republican (Freeport, IL)
Decatur (IL) *Daily Republic*
Decatur (IL) *Herald*
DuQuoin (IL) *Tribune*
Evening Star (Washington, DC)
Fiery Cross (Indianapolis, IN)
Fort Wayne (IN) *Journal Gazette*
Freeport (IL) *Journal Standard*
Illinois State Journal (Springfield)

Indianapolis (IN) *Times*
Inter-Ocean (Chicago)
Ironton (MO) *County Register*
Jonesboro (IL) *Gazette*
Journal Gazette (Mattoon, IL)
Los Angeles Herald
Marion (IL) *Monitor*
Metropolis (IL) *Planet*
Mounds (IL) *Independent*
Mounds (IL) *News*
Murphysboro (IL) *Daily Independent*
National Catholic Welfare Conference News Sheet (New York)
New York Herald
Pantograph (Bloomington, IL)
Pulaski Enterprise (Mound City, IL)
Record (Louisville, KY)
The Republic (Columbus, IN)
San Francisco Call
St. Louis Daily Post-Dispatch
St. Louis Lumberman
St. Louis Republican
The Sun (New York)
Tennessean (Nashville, TN)
The Washington (DC) *Post*
Waterloo (IL) *Evening Courier*

Books

Angle, Paul M. *Bloody Williamson: A Chapter in American Lawlessness.*
New York: Alfred A. Knopf, 1981.

Batinski, Michael C. *Forgetting and the Forgotten: A Thousand Years of Contested Histories in the Heartland.* Carbondale: Southern Illinois University Press, 2021.

Beadles, John A. *Stained with Blood and Tears.* Carbondale, IL: Saluki Press, 2018.

Berg, Manfred. *Popular Justice: A History of Lynching in America.* Chicago: Ivan R. Dee, 2011.

Butler, Lillian Nesbitt. *Living in Cache Bottom.* Self-published, 2005.

Chalmers, David M. *Hooded Americanism: The History of the Ku Klux Klan.*
New York: Franklin Watts, 1951.

Dexter, Darrel. *A History of Beech Grove Church 1900–1998, Rural Ullin, Alexander County, Illinois.* Self-Published, 2015.

Dixon, Thomas Jr. *The Clansman: An Historical Romance of the Ku Klux Klan.*
New York: Doubleday, Page, 1905.

———. *The Leopard's Spots: A Romance of the White Man's Burden: 1865–1900.*
New York: Doubleday, Page, 1902.

———. *The Traitor: A Story of the Fall of the Invisible Empire.* New York: Grosset & Dunlap, 1907.

Dray, Philip. *At the Hands of Persons Unknown: The Lynching of Black America.*
New York: Random House, 2002.

Erwin, Milo. *The Bloody Vendetta of Southern Illinois.* Marion, IL: IllinoisHistory .com, 2006.

Galligan, George. *In Bloody Williamson: My Four Years Fight with the Ku Klux Klan.* Williamson County Historical Society, 1927, reprint 1985.

Gordon, Linda. *The Second Coming of the KKK: The Ku Klux Klan of the 1920s and the American Political Tradition.* New York: Liveright Publishing Corporation, 2017.

Jackson, Kenneth T. *The Ku Klux Klan in the City, 1915–1930.* Chicago: Ivan R. Dee, 1992.

Kloran: White Book Knights of the Ku Klux Klan, 5th ed. Atlanta, GA: Ku Klux Klan Press, 1916.

Lantz, Herman. *A Community in Search of Itself: A Case History of Cairo, Illinois.*
Carbondale: Southern Illinois University Press, 1972.

Loewen, James W. *Sundown Towns: A Hidden Dimension of America.* New York: Simon & Schuster, 2005.

Logan, Rayford. *The Negro in American Life and Thought: The Nadir, 1877–1901.*
New York: Dial Press, 1954.

Lynching in America: Confronting the Legacy of Racial Terror. Equal Justice Initiative, 2015.

McVeigh, Rory. *The Rise of the Ku Klux Klan: Right-Wing Movements and National Politics.* Minneapolis: University of Minnesota Press, 2009.

McWhirter, Cameron. *Red Summer: The Summer of 1919 and the Awakening of Black America.* New York: St. Mary's Griffin, 2011.

Moyers, William N. *Brief History of Pulaski County, 1843–1943.* Mound City, IL: Pulaski Enterprise, 1943.

Official Records of the War of the Rebellion, Series 2, Vol. 5. Washington, DC: Government Printing Office, 1899.

Pegram, Thomas R. *One Hundred Percent American: The Rebirth and Decline of the Klan in the 1920s.* Chicago: Ivan R. Dee, 2011.

Perrin, William Henry, ed. *A History of Alexander, Union and Pulaski Counties, Illinois.* Chicago: O. L. Baski, 1883.

Pfeifer, Michael J. *Rough Justice and American Society 1874–1947.* Urbana: University of Illinois Press, 2004.

Pulaski County Illinois 1819–1987. Paducah, KY: Turner, 1987.

Rushdy, Ashraf H. A. *American Lynching.* New Haven: Yale University Press, 2012.

Shevitz, Amy Hill. *Jewish Communities on the Ohio River: A History.* Lexington: University Press of Kentucky, 2007.

Smith, George Washington. *A History of Southern Illinois*, Vol. 2. Chicago: Lewis, 1912.

Sneed, Glenn J. *Ghost Towns of Southern Illinois.* Johnston City, IL: A.E.R.P., 1977.

Sutherland, John MacLeod. *Then Cometh the Devil.* Butler, IN: Luther H. Higley, 1907.

Wade, Wyn Craig. *The Fiery Cross: The Ku Klux Klan in America.* New York: Oxford University Press, 1998.

Wheeler, Joanne. "Together in Egypt: A Pattern of Race Relations in Cairo, Illinois, 1865–1915." In *Toward a New South*, edited by Orville Vernon Burton and Robert C. McMath Jr., 265–284. Westport, CT: Greenwood Press, 1982.

Williams, Erma Brooks. *Political Empowerment of Illinois' African American State Lawmakers from 1877 to 2005.* Lanham, MD: University Press of America, 2008.

Young, J. M. *Cairo Illustrated.* Cairo, IL: E. E. and C. M. Ellis, 1903.

Journal and Magazine Articles

Ayabe, Masatomo. "Ku Kluxers in a Coal Mining Community: A Study of the Ku Klux Klan Movement in Williamson County, Illinois, 1923–1926."

Journal of the Illinois State Historical Society 102, no. 1 (Spring 2009): 73–100.

Carlson, Shirley J. "Black Migration to Pulaski County 1860–1900." *Illinois Historical Journal* 80, no. 1 (Spring 1986): 37–46.

Hall, Andy. "The Ku Klux Klan in Southern Illinois in 1875," *Journal of the Illinois State Historical Society* 46, no. 4 (Winter 1953): 363–372.

Inscore, John C. "The Clansman on Stage and Screen." *North Carolina Historical Review* 64, no. 2 (April 1987): 139–161.

Raines, Edgar F. Jr. "The Ku Klux Klan in Illinois, 1867–1875." *Illinois Historical Journal* 78, no. 1 (Spring 1985): 17–44.

Unpublished Manuscripts

William Fletcher McMurry Papers 1885–1934, 3487. State Historical Society of Missouri. Folders 67, 69, and 71.

Theses and Dissertations

Ayabe, Masatoma. "The Ku Klux Klan Movement in Williamson County, Illinois, 1923–1926." PhD diss., University of Illinois, Urbana, 2005.

Peterson, Hannah Bethann. *Murder at Mer Rouge: A Dialogue on the Activities of the Ku Klux Klan in Northwestern Louisiana, 1921–1924.* Fellows thesis, Texas A & M University, 2004. http://oaktrust.library.tamu.edu/bitstream/handle /1969.1/ETD-TAMU-2004-FELLOWS-THESIS-P45/2004%20Fellows% 20Thesis%20P45.pdf.

Interviews

Shawnee Community College Local History Project, Owen Evers, July 16, 1975.
Shawnee Community College Local History Project, Warner Wall, October 10, 1975.

Internet

Black Then: Discovering Our History, https://blackthen.com/today-in-1906 -thousands-of-blacks-protested-against-the-clansman-stage-play -in-philadelphia/. Accessed July 26, 2022.

Dunphy, John J. "A Brief History of the Ku Klux Klan in Southwestern Illinois," medium.com/@johnjdunphy/a-brief-history-of-the-ku-klux-klan -in-southwestern -illinois-ca2b17ee3d67. Accessed May 14, 2021.

"Lynchings by Year and Race," University of Missouri Kanas City Law School, http://law2.umkc.edu/faculty/projects/ftrials/shipp/lynchingyear.html. Accessed May 21, 2022.

McClellan McAndrew, Tara. "History: The 1920s Saw the KKK Rise in Illinois," nprillinois.org/post/history-1920s-saw-kkks-rise-illinois.

"Prices Received for Corn—Dollars Per Bushel," U.S. Department of Agriculture, National Agricultural Statistics Service, https://www.nass.usda.gov/Statistics _by_State/Washington/Publications/Historic_Data/fieldcrops/cornprc.pdf. Accessed July 18, 2022.

United States Census Bureau, https://www.census.gov/population/cencounts /il190090.txt.

U.S. Census, Georgia, https://www2.census.gov/library/publications/decennial /1920/volume-3/41084484v3ch03.pdf. Accessed February 12, 2022.

City Directories

Cairo Illinois City Directory, Vol. VI, 1922–1923, Asheville, NC: The Miller Press, July 1922.

Daily Telegram's Cairo City Directory for 1904, Cairo, IL: E. E. and C. M. Ellis, 1904.

Polk-Gould 1925 St. Louis Directory. https://stlouis.genealogyvillage.com/1925churches .htm. Accessed January 6, 2022.

Pamphlets

Evans, J. A., J. C. Hackleman, and F. C. Bauer. "Cotton Growing in Illinois," University of Illinois Agricultural College and Experiment Station, Urbana IL, March 1924, Circular 279.

Gardner, Samuel Patrick. *Up from Slavery and Fifty Years a Teacher in the Schools of Southern Illinois*, Vienna, IL: A. B. Thacker, n.d.

Ku Klux Klan: A Report to the Illinois General Assembly, Illinois Legislative Investigating Commission, Chicago: State of Illinois, October 1976.

Government Census Records

Fifteenth Census of the United States: 1930, Population, Volume III, Part 1, Alabama-Missouri. U.S. Government Printing Office, Washington, DC, 1932.

Fourteenth Census of the United States Taken in the Year 1920, Population 1920, Number and Distribution of Inhabitants, Vol. 1. Government Printing Office, Washington, DC, 1921.

Illinois State Archives Records

Alexander County, Illinois, Court Records.

Alexander County, Illinois, Criminal Record Book 30.

Alexander County Coroner's Record Book.

Alexander County Criminal Record Book, People v. Fred Kenner, Henry Metcalf, and William Slauson, Case No. 2360.

People v. Harry Winters, et al, Indictment, a True Bill, Case No. 1267 (Secretary of State Index Division: Executive Section. Petitions for Requisitions to the Governor, 1867–1949, Illinois State Archives).

Pulaski County, Illinois, Circuit Court Book 14.

Pulaski County, Illinois, Circuit Court Book 21.

Pulaski County, Illinois, Court Records.

Secretary of State (Index Division), Executive Session, Petitions for Requisitions to the Governor, 1867–1949, Illinois State Archives (libraryhost.com), series 103.088, 103.063, 103090.

INDEX

Page numbers in italics indicate illustrations.

African Methodist Episcopal Church
(Mound City), 121
Age of Lynching, 4
Albright, Fountaine E., 35
Alexander, Arthur, 102
Alexander County, IL, 50; agriculture
in, 48; Black political power limited,
12–14; bootlegging in, 51–52, 90,
134, 150n16; cotton production in,
87–88; First Ku Klux Klan in,
30–32; importance of railroads in,
49; lumber industry in, 49; parts
hostile to Black residency, 6; and
Second Ku Klux Klan, 16, 135–36
Americanism, as defined by Second Ku
Klux Klan, 59, 61
Amnesty Act of 1872, 29–30
Anderson, William Paul, 57, 136,
167n25; farewell address, 136;
impersonation by mob member,
108–9; relocation to Florida, 136;
swearing in as deputy, 108
Anna, IL, hostility to Black residency
in, 37, 83, 86
anti-Catholicism. *See* Second Ku Klux
Klan.
anti-Semitism. *See* Second Ku Klux
Klan.
Anton, Joseph J., 67
Arnold, Carl, 120

Assumption Christian Church (Pana),
152n17
Atherton, Harvey Beachum, 61

Bailey, Fred. *See* Hale, Fred
Ballard County, KY, 84, 127, 129
Barlow, KY, 127
Barr, William W., 35
Bass, Liston D., 24, 145n38
Beasley, Dora Thompson, 87–88, 157n39
Beasley, William R., 87
Beech Grove Methodist Episcopal
Church (Alexander County), 1–2,
61–62
Behme, Fred, 120
Belknap, Charles Leroy, 60–61
Bell, Bob, 101
Belleville, IL, 66–67
Belt, Logan, 36, 148n36
Benton, IL, 46, 124
Bethea, Rainey, 121
Bettis, Mary C., 25–26
Betts, Lark Jackson, 90
Beveridge, John Lourie, 34–35, 38
Biden, Joseph R., 131
Bingham, John, 101
Birger, Charlie, 42; execution of, 124
Birth of a Nation, The (1915 Griffith
film), 40; opposition in Mound
City, 68; showing in Anna, 68

DARREL DEXTER is the author of several books, including *Bondage in Egypt: Slavery in Southern Illinois*. He is also the editor of *Stained with Blood and Tears: Lynchings, Murder and Mob Violence in Cairo, Illinois, 1909–1910*. He has taught at the Egyptian Community School in Tamms, Illinois, for 20 years.

JOHN A. BEADLES is the author of *A History of Southernmost Illinois* and *Stained with Blood and Tears: Lynchings, Murder and Mob Violence in Cairo, Illinois, 1909–1910*. He began his teaching career at high schools: Lakeview in Decatur, Illinois; Pontiac Township in Pontiac, Illinois; and Bishop DuBourg in St. Louis, Missouri. He has also taught at Syracuse University, Cazenovia College for Women, Lane College/United Negro College Fund, the State University of New York (Geneseo), St. Louis Community College (Meramec), and Kennesaw State University (Georgia).